D0734301

EUCHARIST

EUCHARIST

ROBERT BARRON

WORD ON FIRE
INSTITUTE

Published by the Word on Fire Institute, an imprint of
Word on Fire, Park Ridge, IL 60068
© 2021 by Word on Fire Catholic Ministries
Printed in the United States of America
All rights reserved.

Cover design, typesetting, and interior art direction
by Rozann Lee and Cassie Pease.

Unless otherwise indicated, Church Father quotes adapted from *Nicene and Post-Nicene Fathers*, Second Series, edited by Philip Schaff and Henry Wace (Buffalo, NY: Christian Literature Publishing Co., 1894). Quotes from Thomas Aquinas' *Summa theologiae* adapted from *The Summa Theologiæ of St. Thomas Aquinas, Second and Revised Edition*, translated by the Fathers of the English Dominican Province (orig. 1920, copyright © 2017). Revised and edited for NewAdvent.org by Kevin Knight. Used by permission.

Excerpts from the English translation of the *Catechism of the Catholic Church* for use in the United States of America Copyright © 1994, United States Catholic Conference, Inc.—Libreria Editrice Vaticana. Used by permission. English translation of the *Catechism of the Catholic Church*: Modifications from the Editio Typica copyright © 1997, United States Conference of Catholic Bishops—Libreria Editrice Vaticana.

Unless otherwise indicated, Scripture quotations are from the New Revised Standard Version Bible: Catholic Edition (copyright © 1989, 1993), used by permission of the National Council of the Churches of Christ in the United States of America. All rights reserved worldwide.

No part of this book may be used or reproduced in any manner whatsoever without written permission, except in the case of brief quotations in critical articles or reviews. For more information, contact Word on Fire, PO Box 170, Des Plaines, IL 60016 or email contact@wordonfire.org.

First Edition published 2008 by Orbis Books.
Second Edition 2021.

24 23 22 21   2 3 4

ISBN: 978-1-943243-82-2

Library of Congress Control Number: 2020925927

CONTENTS

BABETTE'S FEAST

In the Spring of 2007, I was privileged to be a scholar in residence at the North American College in Rome. During that period, I had the opportunity, on three occasions, to distribute communion at Mass in St. Peter's Square. Standing on one side of a partition, I watched as scores of people came forward to receive the Eucharist. In the typically Italian style, things were a tad disorganized, and the faithful were compelled, in the press of the crowd, to stretch out their hands toward me. I saw all sorts of hands—old and young, dirty and clean, lined and unlined—reaching out for the Bread of Life. When I would move along the partition, some would cry out to me plaintively, "Padre, Padre, per favore" (Father, Father, please). Never before in my priesthood, though I had distributed communion to thousands, had I had the sense of carrying food to those who were desperate for it. Those faithful in St. Peter's Square embodied a truth that is deep in our Catholic tradition, though too infrequently stated: the Eucharist is not a luxury but a necessity, for without it we would, in the spiritual sense, starve to death.[1]

The fathers of the Second Vatican Council expressed this truth in a lyrical and oft-repeated phrase from the document *Lumen Gentium*: the Eucharistic sacrifice is "the fount and apex" (or, as another translation has it, "the source and summit") of the whole Christian life.[2] It is both the fountain from which life in Christ flows and the goal toward which

---

1. This image was suggested to me in a marvelous sermon preached at the North American College by Fr. James Quigley, OP, in the spring of 2007.

2. *Lumen Gentium*, no. 11, in *The Word on Fire Vatican II Collection* (Park Ridge, IL: Word on Fire Institute, 2021), 59.

it tends; it is the alpha and the omega of Christian discipleship; it is the energy without which authentic Christianity runs down. Without the Eucharist, we could be a pious congregation of like-minded people or a society dedicated to the memory and teaching of Jesus, but we couldn't possibly be the Church. As John Paul II argued in what was, fittingly enough, his last encyclical, *Ecclesia de Eucharistia* (the Church comes from the Eucharist), the Body and Blood of Jesus are not simply the sacred objects at the center of the Church's concern; they *are* the Church, its lifeblood and raison d'être.

In one of his sermons on the Eucharist, the great English Catholic preacher Ronald Knox made the following observation. The vast majority of Jesus' commands—to love one's enemies, to turn the other cheek, to forgive seventy times seven times, etc.—have been rather consistently disregarded. (As Chesterton pointed out, it is not that Christianity has been tried and found wanting, but rather that it has been found difficult and never tried.[3]) However, Knox says, amid all of these commandments honored, at best, in the breach, there is one command of Jesus that has, up and down the centuries, been massively obeyed. Throughout the long history of the Church, through a whole series of dramatic successes and failures, despite the stupidity and wickedness of so many Christians, the command "Do this in memory of me" has been and continues to be obeyed. It is as though Christians, in all of their sin, have realized from the beginning that the spiritual life depends upon the Eucharist the way that physical life depends upon food, oxygen, and water. And so, almost despite themselves, they do what Jesus told them to do in his memory.

The topic of the Eucharist is huge and multivalent. Thousands of treatises, essays, sermons, and reflections have been dedicated to it over the centuries. Its mysteries and dimensions are endless precisely because the Eucharist *is* Christ, the one in whom, according to Paul, are hidden all the treasures of wisdom and knowledge. One could easily construct

---

3. See G.K. Chesterton, *What's Wrong with the World* (New York: Dodd & Mead, 1910), 48.

an entire systematic theology around the central motif of the Eucharist, showing how it is intimately related to the doctrines of creation, revelation, Christology, grace, redemption, and the last things. However, I am going to follow the lead of many Eucharistic commentators and focus on three major themes: meal, sacrifice, and Real Presence.

The Eucharist is, first, the great meal of fellowship that God wants to establish with his people, the joyful bond in which the divine life is shared spiritually and physically with a hungry world. However—and this will emerge as a major argument of this book—communion in a fallen world is impossible without sacrifice. In a universe that has become twisted and off-kilter, beset by division, hatred, and fear, the establishment of real love and justice will come only at the price of suffering. Hence, the Eucharist is also the embodiment of Jesus' great act of sacrificial suffering on the cross at Calvary; in the separate consecration of the bread and the wine, we see, symbolically expressed, the separation of Christ's body and blood that took place in the process of his dying. What we eat and drink at the fellowship meal, therefore, is nothing other than the death of Jesus, the act by which he gave himself away for the salvation of the world. And both of these themes are gathered up and given full expression in the Catholic doctrine of the *Real* Presence of Jesus in the Eucharistic elements. Though it contains a symbolic dimension, the Eucharist is more than a symbol, more than a concoction, however moving and evocative, of our own religious imagination. In it, Jesus is present to us through his own power and in his dense objectivity as both food and sacrificial offering. There is something terrible and uncontrollable in the *reality* of this presence. The Eucharist is not our product but our Lord, and as such, it calls us to conversion. The rest of this book will be a further elaboration of the three themes that I have just sketched.

I should like to begin, not with doctrine or liturgical practice or theological arguments, but rather with a story, since, as usual, the poets say it best.

Babette's Feast

In 1956, the Danish writer Isak Dinesen (the pen name of Karen Blixen) published a short story called "Babette's Feast," which, many years later, provided the basis for an extremely popular film. Dinesen's story is about many things—friendship, loss, religious devotion, sensual delight, loyalty—but it is, I think, primarily about the Eucharist. In fact, I know of no other literary text that so fully expresses the complex of themes that cluster around this central Christian mystery.

The narrative is set in the late nineteenth century in a remote village nestled at the foot of a mountain at the edge of a Norwegian fjord. Two sisters—Martine and Philippa—the daughters of a revered Lutheran pastor who had founded an ardent sect of followers, preside over the small community. Though these disciples of the "Dean" were still admired throughout the country, their numbers were diminishing and the remaining adepts were getting "whiter, balder, and harder of hearing." The great mark of this austere fellowship was puritanism, the conviction that earthly joys had to be set aside if the journey toward the heavenly Jerusalem was to be facilitated. They would eat the simplest meals and live in the most frugal surroundings so that they would be free to help the poor and give themselves to prayer. We hear that Martine and Philippa have a maid called Babette.

When they were young women, both sisters were remarkably beautiful and accordingly attracted a number of suitors. But when prospective husbands would come forward seeking the Dean's permission, the old man would respond that his daughters were "his right and left hand"[4] and thus indispensable to him. Indeed, the girls themselves had accepted an "ideal of heavenly love" and therefore "did not let themselves be touched by the flames of this world."[5] Nevertheless, in their youth

---

4. Isak Dinesen, "Babette's Feast," in *Anecdotes of Destiny and Ehrengard* (New York: Vintage International, 1993), 22.

5. Dinesen, 22–23.

both were beguiled by romantic possibilities. In 1854, when Martine was eighteen, a dashing military officer named Lorens Löwenhielm presented himself at the Dean's home and was immediately smitten by the young woman. He followed her about, sought her out, visited her home, but became hopelessly tongue-tied and self-conscious around the Dean's table, incapable of communicating his feelings. He loved her, but he knew that he would never be able to break down the wall of pious reserve that she had constructed around herself. Finally, on the day before he was due to leave, Martine showed him to the door. In his desperation he grabbed her hand, pressed it to his lips, and uttered, "I am going away forever! I shall never, never see you again! For I have learned here that Fate is hard, and that in this world there are things which are impossible."[6] Upon returning home, he resolved to forget about romance and to concentrate upon the cultivation of his military career.

A year later, an even more distinguished person came to the small town. Achille Papin, one of the most impressive opera singers of the time, had spent a week with the Royal Opera of Stockholm. He had heard of the ravishing beauty of the Norwegian coast and decided to see it on his way back to France. On a Sunday he wandered into the small church of the Dean's congregation and heard Philippa sing. The girl had a voice so glorious that Papin became convinced that the music world of Paris would be at her feet. Through the sheer force of his personality, he managed to secure the Dean's permission and commenced to work with Philippa. His original intuitions were confirmed in the course of the lessons, and he predicted that soon she would be the finest singer of her time: "My greatest triumphs are before me! The world will once more believe in miracles when she and I sing together!"[7] So ecstatic would be her reception that nobles and ladies in Paris would conduct her, after her performance, to the finest restaurant in the city, the

6. Dinesen, 24.
7. Dinesen, 27.

Café Anglais, where a sumptuous supper would be spread before her. During one of their sessions, Achille and Philippa sang the "seduction duet" from Mozart's *Don Giovanni*. As the last notes faded into the air, the master took his disciple in his arms and kissed her. Immediately afterward, Philippa asked her father to write to M. Papin, informing him that she wanted no further vocal lessons. Heartbroken, the great singer returned to France on the first boat, convinced that something irrevocable had been lost.

Fifteen years later, the bell-rope of the sisters' home was violently pulled. When they opened the door, they found a pale, frightened woman who, upon taking one step inside, fell into a dead swoon. When she came around, the mysterious visitor produced a letter, written in French and signed by Achille Papin. It served as an introduction to the woman who stood trembling and anxious before them: Babette Hersant. She had been, Papin explained, a *pétroleuse* during the recent communard uprising in Paris and had lost both her husband and her son in the fighting. Unable to remain in France, she was seeking, at Papin's suggestion, refuge with the kind sisters whom he had known so many years before. He closed the letter with the tossed-off remark: "Babette can cook."[8] In great generosity of spirit, the sisters took in this forlorn character, and in time, in the friendly surroundings of their household, Babette "acquired all the appearance of a respectable and trusted servant."[9] Because they were suspicious of French cooking (the French, they had heard, ate frogs), they taught Babette how to prepare their customary meal of split cod and ale-and-bread soup. Given their religious commitments, they explained, their food must be as plain as possible. Luxury at the table they considered an immoral extravagance. Though she never mastered Norwegian and though she remained something of an enigma to the people of the village, Babette was eventually accepted as a respected member of the community.

---

8. Dinesen, 30.
9. Dinesen, 31.

We learn (returning to the present day) that the one hundredth anniversary of the Dean's birth is approaching and that the sisters want to do something special to celebrate the date. Even as they contemplate this happy prospect, they are chagrined that the spirit of their father seemed to have dissipated among his followers, for "discord and dissension had been raising their heads in his flock."[10] The essential problem, expressed in a variety of ways and contexts, was the inability to forgive. Martine and Philippa vaguely hoped that the upcoming festivity would bring the spiritual family together again. As they were considering how best to mark the great day, a letter arrived from France for Babette, containing the improbable news that she had won ten thousand francs in the national lottery. Soon after, Babette begged the sisters to let her cook a celebratory dinner in honor of the Dean's birthday. This suggestion took them aback, for though they intended to celebrate the day, they had no intention of sponsoring a festive dinner. But their cook was so insistent and eager in her pleading that eventually they gave in. And Babette had more to say: she wanted to cook for their guests, not the simple, unappetizing fare to which they were accustomed, but a real, sumptuous French dinner; and she wanted to pay for it herself. When the sisters balked, Babette stepped forward with great and even frightening resolve and said, "Ladies! Have I ever, during twelve years, asked you a favor? No! And why not? . . . What would I have had to pray for? Nothing! Tonight I have a prayer to make, from the bottom of my heart."[11] Their resistance broke down, and they granted her request.

A month before the feast, Babette went on a journey (her first in twelve years). When she returned, she announced that the goods necessary for the dinner were ordered and on their way. Though the very idea of elaborate preparations for a meal, requiring a journey to a

---

10. Dinesen, 34.
11. Dinesen, 38 (slightly adapted for clarity).

foreign country, was preposterous to the sisters, they "gave themselves into their cook's hands."[12] During the next days, the food, drink, and other accoutrements began to arrive. They were surprised by the numerous bottles of wine, each with a label carefully providing its name and point of origin (Martine never dreamed that wines could have names!); but they were flabbergasted beyond words by the enormous and primordial-looking turtle that poked its snake-like head out of its greenish-black shell. The sisters began to fear that, in surrendering to the wishes of their French cook, they were making their father's house into the setting for a witch's sabbath. When Martine and Philippa communicated these fears to their friends and neighbors, everyone agreed that they would eat the French meal out of deference to Babette but that, as a protest, they would not speak of it nor take any pleasure in it. One of the white-bearded elders said, "On the day of our master we will cleanse our tongues of all taste and purify them of all delight or disgust of the senses, keeping and preserving them for the higher things of praise and thanksgiving."[13]

The great dinner took place on Sunday, the Lord's Day. The first guest to arrive was old Mrs. Loewenhielm, who, at ninety, had lost practically all of her hearing and sense of taste, and who was, as such, the embodiment of the community's puritanical indifference to the pleasures of this world. She was escorted by her nephew, General Loewenhielm, the man who as a young officer so many years before had sought unsuccessfully to court Martine. He happened to be visiting his aunt at this time, and the old lady, concerned about his listless spirits, had pressed the sisters to invite him. Though he had achieved all of his worldly goals, satisfying all of his career ambitions, the general felt unaccountably depressed and came to the dinner only reluctantly. In time, the other guests arrived, until the drawing room was filled with twelve celebrants. One very old brother, in his

12. Dinesen, 39.
13. Dinesen, 41.

trembling voice, then began to sing a hymn that had been composed by the Dean himself:

Jerusalem, my happy home
name ever dear to me.[14]

Gradually, the guests took up the well-known tune, and as they sang, they joined hands in fellowship. So caught up were they in the spirit of the moment that they took up a second hymn and, hands still joined, sang it through to the end.

After this impromptu choral prelude, they entered the dining room, where they saw the table elegantly prepared, the glasses and silverware gleaming in the light from a row of flickering candles. When everyone was seated, one of the elders recited the lovely grace that the Dean had given them:

May my food my body maintain,
may my body my soul sustain,
may my soul in deed and word
give thanks for all things to the Lord.[15]

Then they all commenced to eat and drink. General Loewenhielm, the only guest at the table who had not vowed to take no sensual delight in the meal, now wore a puzzled expression. For the wine he was sipping was (he could barely believe it) "Amontillado! And the finest Amontillado that I have ever tasted."[16] And the soup was turtle soup—the best he had ever had. Then a new dish was served, and as everyone quietly ate, the general thought to himself, "It is Blinis Demidoff!"[17] But when he tasted the main course, his

14. Dinesen, 43.
15. Dinesen, 48.
16. Dinesen, 48.
17. Dinesen, 49.

astonishment was complete. Many years before, at the Café Anglais, he had eaten "an incredibly recherché and palatable dish"[18] called Cailles en Sarcophage, which had been invented by the chef of that establishment. Turning to the man on his left, the general said, "But this is Cailles en Sarcophage!" Having no idea what the general was talking about, the man said, with utter blandness, "Yes, Yes, certainly. What else would it be?"[19] As the meal progressed, something strange and wonderful was happening. As stories of the Dean were exchanged and as the fine food and wine gradually were having their effect, old animosities were melting away, old resentments were being healed, broken friendships were being repaired. A spirit of forgiveness and good cheer seemed to take hold of all those around the table.

So moved by what he had experienced at the banquet, and still regretting his tongue-tied self-consciousness in this same home so many years before, General Loewenhielm rose to speak. He himself was surprised by the words that came out of his mouth, for though he had been formally trained to give commands and orations on drill grounds and in royal halls, he now felt that he was but a vehicle for a higher presence. "In our human foolishness and short-sightedness," he said, "we imagine that grace is finite. . . . But the moment comes when our eyes are opened and we realize that grace is infinite. Grace, my friends," he went on, "demands nothing of us but that we shall await it with confidence and acknowledge it in gratitude. . . . Grace takes us all to its bosom and proclaims general amnesty."[20] In the wake of this extraordinary oration, the entire place seemed suffused with the very grace that the general spoke of: "The rooms had been filled with a heavenly light, as if a number of small halos had blended into one glorious radiance. Taciturn old people received the gift of tongues; ears that for years had been almost deaf were opened to it. Time itself

---

18. Dinesen, 50.
19. Dinesen, 51.
20. Dinesen, 52.

had merged into eternity."[21] All during the meal, it had snowed, so that when the guests were taking their leave, they noticed the entire countryside blanketed in white. As they set out, they staggered and wavered on their feet, slipping and sliding in the snow. Some slipped down or fell forward, so that their elbows, backsides, and knees were covered in white, and as they walked away, they were "gamboling like little lambs."[22]

But the story does not end on this gentle note, all things simply reconciled, all enemies simply forgiven. Our attention shifts to the kitchen, so that we can see the price that was paid to make this mystical, grace-filled gathering possible. We are told, bluntly enough, that "Babette alone had had no share in the bliss of the evening."[23] Like a sacrificial victim, "Babette sat on the chopping block,"[24] surrounded by a plethora of greasy pots and pans, as exhausted and deadly white as she had been on the night when the sisters first took her in. After twelve years of silence on this point, she then spoke her identity: "I was once cook at the Café Anglais."[25] This meant little to the sisters, but Babette continued, laying out to them the full extent of her sacrifice. Her husband and son were gone—lost, as we have heard, in the communard uprising—but gone too were the whole bevy of gentlemen and aristocrats who used to frequent the Café Anglais. Babette's world had disappeared. Moreover, she said, "I have no money."[26] When the sisters protested that she had just won the French lottery, Babette calmly explained that she had spent every centime of her winnings on the great dinner.

This summary that I have presented can barely hint at the artistry in Dinesen's beautifully understated narrative, but it can serve at least

---

21. Dinesen, 53.
22. Dinesen, 54.
23. Dinesen, 55.
24. Dinesen, 56.
25. Dinesen, 56.
26. Dinesen, 56.

as a framework for discussing the Eucharistic symbolism that suffuses the story. The fundamental motif is that the gracefulness of the meal is interwoven with, and made possible by, a whole series of sacrifices, most notably Babette's. We recall that the Dean's congregation is characterized by a rather marked dualism or puritanism, according to which the things of God are divorced from the affairs and pleasures of this world. Though it has haunted the Christian tradition from the beginning, this kind of dualism is, in fact, deeply unbiblical. According to the scriptural reading, God is intimately involved in the world that he has made, and every nook and cranny of creation speaks of the beauty of the Creator. Accordingly, the biblical imagination is not dualist, but sacramental. Though the world is other than God, the world serves as an icon of the one who made it, and therefore, whatever is good, true, and beautiful in creation functions as a potential point of contact between human beings and God. In their conviction that the heavenly Jerusalem is attained only through the eschewing of the pleasures of this world, in their exaggerated asceticism, the Dean's congregation had lost sight of this basic truth. In fact, the very sadness and dwindling size of the community could be seen as consequences of this forgetfulness. One of the most poignant features of the story is that this dualist asceticism extended as far as precluding the sisters from romantic involvement. They had, as we saw, rejected "the flames of this world" in order to give themselves to the service of God, and hence both had turned away from giving themselves in love to a man.

Into this dualist milieu, came, unexpectedly, a visitor from another world. Babette, the master chef accustomed to the highest and finest things, arrived from Catholic France, but she was weak and lonely and bore the haggard look of a beggar. This is our first clue that the exiled cook is a figure of Christ. In his Letter to the Philippians, Paul said that Christ, "though he was in the form of God . . . emptied himself, taking the form of a slave, being born in the likeness of men" (Phil. 2:6–7). Christ left his natural dwelling place and willingly entered into the limitations of our world in order to transfigure it by his presence. Paul comments, in a similar vein, that by his poverty, we became rich (see 2 Cor. 8:9). Dinesen says, in the very cadences of Paul, that though Babette "appeared to be a beggar . . . she turned out to be a conquerer."[27] But the transformation that she effects is not an immediate one. Rather, it is prepared for by a long period of humble identification with those to whom she was sent. Although she was one of the finest chefs in Europe, she willingly agreed to prepare the simplest and least appetizing of meals; although she was used to mingling with the elite of French society, she acquiesced to making the rounds of an obscure Norwegian fishing village. But all the while, clandestinely, secretly, she is having her effect: "Her quiet countenance and her steady, deep glance had magnetic qualities; under her eyes things moved, noiselessly, into their proper places."[28] In a word, Babette's humble self-emptying was remaking a disordered world from within.

But we see the full extent of this sacrifice and this remaking only in regard to the great meal. It is a biblical commonplace that God desires to express his intimacy with his people through a festive meal. In the prophet Isaiah, we find wonderful images of a great feast that God will host on the summit of the holy mountain. There will be, we are told, "rich food filled with marrow" and "well-aged wines" (Isa. 25:6). In the book of Wisdom, moreover, God is pictured as a Jewish mother spreading a sumptuous feast before her people. A meal at which the good things of this world become evocative of the divine presence, and at which brothers and sisters sit down in intimacy with God and one another, is a consistent biblical symbol of what God wants for us. It is absolutely no accident that Jesus takes up this theme, embodying it in his ministry of table fellowship. All were welcome around the table of Jesus—the rich and the poor, the respectable and the marginalized, the saint and the sinner, the healthy

---

27. Dinesen, 31.
28. Dinesen, 31.

and the sick. This festive eating and drinking was appreciated by Jesus as an eschatological symbol, as the concrete realization of Isaiah's dream of divine-human fellowship. And at the culminating moment of his life, Jesus sat down with his twelve Apostles and hosted a final meal. Recapitulating the whole of the biblical tradition of the festive meal and summing up the whole of his life and ministry, Jesus fed his Apostles with his very self, offering himself to them in a total sacrifice, dying that they might live: "Take this, all of you, and eat of it, for this is my Body. . . . Take this, all of you, and drink from it, for this is the chalice of my Blood."[29]

And so Babette, as the culmination of her life and work among the people of the village, hosted a meal, which, at the symbolic level, is both the Last Supper and the Mass. It commenced, appropriately enough, on Sunday, the day of the Christian liturgy. As soon as the guests assembled, they sang a hymn, evocative of the opening song of the Mass. They then entered a great dining room and sat at a table bedecked with candles, in the manner of an altar. And at this table, a sumptuous, expensive, delightful meal was served. As they ate and drank, their spirits were uplifted, old memories were stirred, resentments seemed to melt away, forgiveness was offered, and in the words of Martine, "the stars have come nearer."[30] General Loewenhielm's magnificent speech, in which he invoked the infinity of God's grace, named precisely the dynamic of the meal. God (who is nothing but grace) had indeed, through the mediation of the sensual sign of Babette's feast, addressed and blessed his people. Heaven was not, as they had imagined, far away, and in its light, they saw the earth for the first time as it really was. The liturgy is a sacred meal at which God, in sheer graciousness, feeds his people with his own substance, thereby uniting them to him

---

29. *Roman Missal* (ICEL, 2010). See 1 Cor. 11:24–25; Matt. 26:26–28; Mark 14:22–24; Luke 22:19–20.

30. Dinesen, "Babette's Feast," 55.

and to one another, offering the forgiveness of sins, and displaying a new vision of the world.

But then we see that this communion was made possible by a terrible sacrifice. Babette had paid a price, emptying herself out utterly, spending money, talent, and energy in abundance, in order to allow the grace to flow. It is a basic biblical truth—and we will elaborate upon it more fully in the course of the book—that a world gone wrong can be corrected only through sacrifice,[31] that is to say, through an act of love which takes on evil and reworks it from within. In Jerusalem, the night before his death, Jesus indeed hosted a festive meal at which humanity and divinity were reconciled; but at the heart of the feast was sacrifice, the giving away of his Body and Blood. An act of self-negating love made possible the communion that they enjoyed. Like Babette, Jesus situated himself on a chopping block as the festivity unfolded.

There is a rather shocking detail mentioned at the very end of "Babette's Feast." As the dumbfounded sisters were trying to take in the full significance of their maid's gift, Martine remembered a tale that an African missionary had recounted to her father. It seems that the missionary had saved the life of an old chief's favorite wife and, in gratitude, the chief had treated the Christian to a meal. Only many years afterward did the missionary learn from one of his own servants that the main course at the meal had been "a small fat grandchild of the chief's, cooked in honor of the great Christian medicine man." Meal and sacrifice coalesced around the densely textured *reality* of what was offered. Though it repulsed her even to think of it, Martine realized that Babette had effected something very similar, giving herself away as a sacrifice that made possible a meal of grace. So *real* was her gift that it was as though they were eating and drinking her very

---

31. See Matthew Levering, *Sacrifice and Community: Jewish Offering and Christian Eucharist* (Malden, MA: Blackwell, 2005).

15

substance. At the Last Supper, Jesus said, "Take, eat; this is my body" and "Drink from it, all of you; for this is my blood of the covenant" (Matt. 26:26, 27–28). What the disciples are invited to eat *is* the very self that Jesus offers in sacrifice. The grace of communion was so real because the sacrifice of self was so real. In this interweaving of meal, sacrifice, and Real Presence, we discover the heart of a Catholic Eucharistic theology. And therefore these three themes will be the focus of the remainder of this book.

Chapter 1

THE EUCHARIST
AS SACRED MEAL

I would like the images, aromas, and characters of "Babette's Feast" to stay with us as we commence our more technical exploration into the meaning of the Eucharist. John Henry Newman reminded us that the act of religious assent involves much more than acceptance of logical inferences; it is, he argued, as much a matter of hunch, intuition, and feel as of thought.[1] I would be glad, therefore, if you approached the theology of the Eucharist with the symbolic world of Dinesen's tasty story very much in mind.

The Sacred Meal in the Old Testament

We shall begin with the theme of the sacred meal, and we shall set this theme in the widest possible biblical framework. The opening line of the book of Genesis tells us that "in the beginning . . . God created the heavens and the earth" (Gen. 1:1). Why did God, who is perfect in every way and who stands in need of nothing outside of himself, bother to create at all? There are mythologies and philosophies galore—both ancient and modern—that speak of God needing the universe or benefiting from it in some fashion, but Catholic theology has always

---

1. John Henry Newman, *An Essay in Aid of a Grammar of Assent* (Notre Dame, IN: University of Notre Dame Press, 1979) 230–269.

repudiated these approaches and affirmed God's total self-sufficiency. So the question remains: Why did God create? The answer provided by the First Vatican Council gives expression to the mainstream of Catholic theology: God created the heavens and the earth "of his own goodness and almighty power, not for the increase of his own happiness."[2] The ancient theologian Dionysius the Areopagite said that the good, by its very nature, is diffusive of itself.[3] When you are in a good mood, you don't hide yourself away; on the contrary, you tend to effervesce, communicating your joy. God is the supreme good, and hence God is supremely diffusive of himself; the intensity of his joy is such that it overflows into creation.

Now let us take one more step. Love, in the theological sense, is not a feeling or a sentiment, though it is often accompanied by those psychological states. In its essence, love is an act of the will, more precisely, the willing of the good of the other as other.[4] To love is really to want what is good for someone else and then to act on that desire. Many of us are kind, generous, or just, but only so that someone else might return the favor and be kind, generous, or just to us. This is indirect egotism rather than love. Real love is an ecstatic act, a leaping outside of the narrow confines of my needs and desires and an embrace of the other's good for the other's sake. It is an escape from the black hole of the ego, which tends to draw everything around it into itself. In light of this understanding, we can now see that God's creation of the world is a supreme act of love. God, it is true, has no need of anything outside of himself; therefore, the very existence of the universe is proof that it has been *loved* into being—that is to say, desired utterly for its own sake. Moreover, since God is the maker of the heavens and the earth (biblical

---

2. Heinrich Denzinger et al., *Compendium of Creeds, Definitions, and Declarations on Matters of Faith and Morals*, 43rd ed. (San Francisco: Ignatius Press, 2012), no. 3002, 601.

3. *The Divine Names*, in *Pseudo-Dionysius: The Complete Works*, trans. Colm Luibheid (New York: Paulist Press, 1987), chap. 4. See also Thomas Aquinas' discussions of Dionysius' principle in *Summa theologiae* 1.5.4, 1.27.5, 1.73.3, 1-2.1.4, and elsewhere.

4. See Thomas Aquinas, *Summa contra Gentiles* 1.91.2–3, trans. Anton C. Pegis (New York: Hanover House, 1955).

code for "absolutely everything"), all created things must be connected to one another by the deepest bond. Because all creatures—from archangels to atoms—are coming forth here and now from the creative power of God, all are related to each other through the divine center. We are all—whether we like it or not, whether we acknowledge it or not—ontological siblings, members of the same family of creation and sharing the same Father. In the Middle Ages, Francis of Assisi expressed this idea in his "Canticle of Brother Sun," speaking of "Brother Sun" and "Sister Moon," "Brother Fire" and "Sister Water."[5] That was not simply charming poetry but rather exact metaphysics. Everything in the created order—even inanimate objects, even the most distant cosmic force, even realities that I cannot see—is brother and sister to me. We notice how the author of Genesis exults in describing the wide variety of things that God makes, from the light itself to the earth and sea, to all of the trees and plants that grow from the ground, to those lowly beasts that crawl upon it. From ancient times to the present day, the Church has battled the Gnostic heresy, according to which materiality is a lowly or fallen aspect of reality, the product of a lesser god. The book of Genesis—and the Bible as a whole—is fiercely anti-Gnostic. The one Creator God makes all things, pronounces all of them good, and declares the assemblage of creatures *very* good. Therefore, we can say that the universe, in the biblical reading, has been loved into existence by a joyous God and is marked, at every level and in every dimension, by a coinherence, a connectedness and mutuality. As the culmination of creation, God made the first human beings and gave them mastery over the earth: "God blessed them, saying to them: 'Be fertile and multiply. Fill the earth and subdue it. Have dominion over the fish of the sea, the birds of the air, and all the living things that move on the earth'" (Gen. 1:28). We must be careful to interpret this passage correctly, aware of the numerous critiques that have emerged in the last century

---

5. Francis of Assisi, "Canticle of Brother Sun," in *Francis and Clare: The Complete Works*, trans. Regis J. Armstrong and Ignatius C. Brady (Mahwah, NJ: Paulist Press, 1982), 37–39.

or so concerning ecological indifference and a sort of human-centered chauvinism. The "dominion" spoken of in Genesis has nothing to do with domination and should definitely not be construed as a permission for human beings to take advantage of the world that God has created; just the contrary. What God entrusts to Adam and Eve might best be explained through the term "stewardship." They are to care for creation and, if I can put it this way, they are to be the spokespersons for it, appreciating its order with their illuminated minds and giving expression to its beauty with their well-trained tongues. This responsibility is nowhere better represented than in Genesis' account of Adam giving names to all the animals—that is to say, consciously designating the order and relationality of the created world. Human beings were intended to be the means by which the whole earth would give praise to God, returning in love what God had given in love, uniting all things in a great act of worship. This is why it is no accident that Adam is represented in the tradition of rabbinic interpretation as a priest, the one who effects union between God and creation. As he walks with Yahweh in easy friendship in the cool of the evening, Adam is humanity—and by extension, the whole of the cosmos—as it is meant to be, caught up in a loop of grace, creaturely love answering divine love.

Now, what could be a better symbol of this entire theology of creation than the sacred meal, the banquet at which the Creator shares his life with his grateful creatures? Indeed, Genesis tells us that God placed Adam and Eve in the midst of a garden of earthly delights and gave them permission to eat from all of the trees in the garden save one (Gen. 2:15–17). He instructed them, in short, to participate in his life through the joy of eating and drinking. The ranginess and abandon in the Garden of Eden is evocative of God's desire that his creatures flourish to the utmost. The Church Father Irenaeus of Lyons commented that "the glory of God is a human being fully alive."[6]

---

6. Irenaeus, *Against Heresies* 4.20.7, in *Irenaeus on the Christian Faith: A Condensation of* Against Heresies, trans. and ed. James R. Payton Jr. (Eugene, OR: Pickwick, 2011), 116.

But why then the prohibition? Why is the tree of the knowledge of good and evil forbidden to them? The fundamental determination of good and evil remains, necessarily, the prerogative of God alone, since God is, himself, the ultimate good. To seize this knowledge, therefore, is to claim divinity for oneself—and this is the one thing that a creature can never do and thus should never try. To do so is to place oneself in a metaphysical contradiction, interrupting thereby the loop of grace and ruining the *sacrum convivium* (sacred banquet). Indeed, if we turn ourselves into God, then the link that ought to connect us, through God, to the rest of creation is lost, and we find ourselves alone. This is, in the biblical reading, precisely what happens. Beguiled by the serpent's suggestion that God is secretly jealous of his human creatures, Eve and Adam ate of the fruit of the tree of the knowledge of good and evil. They seized at godliness that they might not be dominated by God, and they found themselves, as a consequence, expelled from the place of joy. Moreover, as the conversation between God and his sinful creatures makes plain, this "original" sin entailed that the connection between Adam and Eve and between humanity and the rest of creation is fatally compromised: "The man said, 'The woman whom you gave to be with me, she gave me fruit from the tree, and I ate.' . . . The woman said, 'The serpent tricked me, and I ate'" (Gen. 3:12, 13).

This complex symbolic narrative is meant to explain the nature of sin as it plays itself out across the ages and even now. God wants us to eat and drink in communion with him and our fellow creatures, but our own fear and pride break up the party. God wants us gathered around him in gratitude and love, but our resistance results in scattering, isolation, violence, and recrimination. God wants the sacred meal; we want to eat alone and on our terms.

But the God of the Bible is relentless in his love. He will not rest until this situation is rectified. The whole of the scriptural story, though contained in a wide variety of texts written at different times for different purposes, can be seen as a coherent narrative of God's attempt to restore the fallen creation, to reestablish the joy of the banquet. In the language of the biblical scholar N.T. Wright, much of the Bible is the account of God's "rescue operation" for his sad and compromised creation.[7] The choosing of Abraham, the Exodus of the children of Israel from Egypt, the giving of the Law on Sinai, the victories of David and Solomon, the sending of the prophets, the setting up of the temple—all are moments in the story of liberation. And in the Christian reading, the rescue operation culminates in Jesus, who recapitulates, sums up, the sacred history that preceded him. He is the one to whom Abraham looked; he is final freedom from the slavery of sin; he is the embodiment of the new Law; he is the true successor of David and Solomon; he is the final teller of the divine truth; his body is the new Temple. This entire saga is the story of God's desire to walk once again in friendship with Adam, to sit down once again with the whole of his creation at a great festive banquet.

Let us look a bit more closely at two Old Testament presentations of the sacred meal. At the very center of the Jewish story of salvation is the event of Exodus and Passover. The children of Israel, who had wandered into Egypt during the time of the patriarch Joseph, became, after many centuries, slaves of the Egyptians, compelled to build fortified cities and monuments for the pharaoh. The Church Father Origen provided a symbolic reading of this narrative, according to which the Israelites stand for all of the spiritual and physical powers that God has given to his people, and the pharaoh (and his underlings) stands for sin and the worship of false gods.[8] Sin, the story is telling us, has enslaved the human race, pressing what is best in us into its service, using mind, will, imagination, courage, and creativity in a perverted way. This perversion, in turn, has set us at odds with one

---

7. See, for example, *Simply Christian: Why Christianity Makes Sense* (New York: Harper-One, 2006), 11, 66.

8. Origen of Alexandria, "The Homilies on Exodus," in *Homilies on Genesis and Exodus*, trans. Ronald E. Heine, 227–387 (Washington, DC: The Catholic University of America Press, 1982).

another, prompting the war of all against all. It is from this state of false worship and dissolution that God wishes to free the Israelites, and so he does battle with the pharaoh and his minions. The plagues that God sends should not be interpreted as arbitrary punishments but as the means by which God enters into the spiritual struggle on our behalf. The final plague, according to the narrative, is the killing of the firstborn throughout Egypt. To protect the children of Israel from this disaster, God instructs them to daub their doorposts with the blood of a slaughtered lamb so that when the angel of death comes, he will see the blood and pass over the homes of the Israelites (Exod. 12:1–13). Hence, the feast of *Pesach* or "Passover," one of the most sacred events on the Hebrew calendar.

In the next section of this book, I will return to that sacrificed lamb and its blood, but for now, I want to focus on the meal that accompanied Passover. In the twelfth chapter of the book of Exodus, we hear that God, after announcing what he will do to the firstborn of the Egyptians, told Moses to instruct the entire nation of Israel to celebrate a ritual meal. Each household was to procure a young, un-blemished lamb and to slaughter it in the evening twilight. Then they were to eat its roasted flesh, along with bitter herbs (reminding them of the bitterness of their slavery) and unleavened bread (because they were on the run, unable to wait for the bread to rise). This sacred Passover meal involving the whole nation must become, God commands, "a day of remembrance for you. You shall celebrate it as a festival to the LORD; throughout your generations you shall observe it as a perpetual ordinance" (Exod. 12:14).

The English word "sin" is derived from the German word *Sünde*, which has the sense of "dividing." The closest English relative to *Sünde* would be "sunder." Sin divides and scatters us, since, as we saw, it involves a severing of our relationship with the Creator God through whom alone we find our unity. As he led the Israelites out of slavery (which is to say, bondage to sin), God established a meal that united the whole people, gathering them, in their households, around a common table and a common food. And he declared that this act of unity must be repeated down through the ages as the defining gesture of the Israelite nation. The Passover meal, in a word, was a recovery (however imperfect) of the easy unity and fellowship of the Garden of Eden, God hosting a banquet at which his human creatures share life with him and each other. Though this theme is a bit muted in the Exodus story, the united Israel was intended by God to be a catalyst for the unification of the world. We must recall that the rescue operation is directed to the descendants of Adam and Eve—which is to say, to the whole human race. God chose Israel neither because of their special merits nor for their peculiar advantage, but rather as a vehicle to carry his salvation to the nations. These slave families, gathering in hope and fellowship around a meal of roasted lamb, bitter herbs, and unleavened bread, were, in the biblical reading, the seeds from which the family of God will grow.

The second Old Testament instance of meal symbolism that I would like to examine is found in the book of the prophet Isaiah. Isaiah is one of the greatest poets in the scriptural tradition, and one of his master images, on display throughout his writings, is the holy mountain. In the second chapter of Isaiah, we find this splendid vision: "In days to come, the mountain of the Lord's house shall be established as the highest of the mountains and shall be raised above the hills; all nations shall stream toward it. Many peoples shall come and say, 'Come, let us climb the mountain of the Lord'" (Isa. 2:2–3). The mountain of the Lord's house is Zion, where the temple, the place of right worship, is situated. What Isaiah dreams of here, therefore, is the coming together of all the scattered tribes of Israel, indeed of the world, around the worship of the true God. The division that commenced with the idolatry in the Garden of Eden ("you will be like God, knowing good and evil" [Gen. 3:5]) is healed through a grateful acknowledgement of God's primacy. The distinctive mark of this rightly ordered worship is peace: "For out of Zion shall go forth instruction, and the word of the LORD from Jerusalem. He shall judge between the nations, and shall arbitrate for many peoples; they shall beat their swords into plowshares, and their spears into pruning hooks" (Isa. 2:3–4). Having found friendship with God, Isaiah implies, human beings will rediscover friendship with one another, and they will not feel the need to train for war anymore. The cosmic implication of this reconciliation is made plain in the eleventh chapter of Isaiah, where the prophet dreams of the age of the Messiah. "The wolf shall live with the lamb, the leopard shall lie down with the kid. . . . The cow and the bear shall graze, their young shall lie down together. . . . The weaned child shall put its hand on the adder's den. They will not hurt or destroy on all my holy mountain" (Isa. 11:6–9). We saw that the original sin entailed a falling apart of the whole of God's creation, a setting at enmity of humanity and nature. Here, on the holy mountain, the place of right worship, all is reconciled and reintegrated.

But there is a third and culminating feature of God's holy mountain that Isaiah specially emphasizes. The mountain is the place of right worship and cosmic peace, but it is also the locale of a magnificent meal. In the twenty-fifth chapter, we find this: "On this mountain the LORD of hosts will make for all peoples a feast of rich food, a feast of well-aged wines, of rich food filled with marrow, of well-aged wines strained clear" (Isa. 25:6). In Isaiah's vision, the gathered community is fed by a gracious God with the finest foods, calling to mind the situation in the Garden of Eden before the eating and drinking was interrupted by a grasp at godliness. The prophet envisions all the nations of the world, living in nonviolence and informed by right worship, able to share life with God and one another, receiving and giving grace. We've seen that this holy mountain is Zion, Jerusalem, the place of the temple. In "Babette's Feast," the members of the Dean's community sang often of the heavenly

Jerusalem for which they longed. What they were singing about is precisely what Isaiah is dreaming about: God's festive meal shared with his holy people.

The Sacred Meal in the Life and Ministry of Jesus

For Christians, the most important thing to note about Jesus is that he is not simply one more in a long line of prophets and teachers. He is not merely, like Isaiah, Jeremiah, Moses, or David, a good man who represents God. Rather, he consistently speaks and acts in the very person of God. In the words of N.T. Wright, Jesus is like a portrait of Yahweh, in all of its richness and complexity, sprung to life.[9] When he claims interpretive authority over the Torah, when he forgives the sins of the paralyzed man, when he calls his disciples to love him above mother and father, indeed above their very lives, when he cleanses the temple, Jesus says and does things that only Yahweh could legitimately say and do. In its later creeds and dogmas, the Church expressed this biblical conviction, speaking of Jesus as the Incarnation of the Word of God, as "God from God, Light from Light, true God from true God."[10] Now, we've been arguing that one of the principal desires of Yahweh was to reestablish the sacred meal, to restore the community and fellowship lost through sin. Thus, it should be no surprise that Jesus would make the sacred meal central to his messianic work. Throughout his public ministry, Jesus gathered people around a table of fellowship. In the Palestine of his time, the table was a place where the divisions and stratifications of the society were particularly on display, but at Jesus' table, all were welcome: saints and sinners, the just and the unjust, the healthy and the sick, men and women. This open-table fellowship was not simply a challenge to the societal status quo, but also an

---

9. N.T. Wright, "Jesus and the Identity of God," *Ex Auditu* 14 (January 1998): 42–56.
10. *Roman Missal* (ICEL, 2010).

expression of God's deepest intentions vis-à-vis the human race, the realization of Isaiah's eschatological dream. In fact, very often, Jesus' profoundest teachings took place at table, calling to mind Isaiah's holy mountain where a festive meal would be spread out and where "instruction" would go forth.

Let us examine just a few instances of this meal fellowship in the New Testament, beginning in a perhaps surprising place: the story of Christmas. The account of Jesus' birth in the Gospel of Luke is not, as Raymond E. Brown reminded us, an innocent tale that we tell to children.[11] Instead, all of the drama and edginess of the story of Jesus are adumbrated there. We are meant to notice a contrast between the figure mentioned at the outset of the narrative—Caesar Augustus— and the character who is at the center of the story. Caesar would have been the best-fed person in the ancient world, able at the snap of his fingers to have all of his sensual desires met. But the true king, the true emperor of the world, is born in a cave outside of a forgotten town on the verge of Caesar's domain. Too weak even to raise his head, he is wrapped in swaddling clothes and then laid "in a manger," the place where the animals eat (Luke 2:7). What Luke is signaling here is that Jesus had come to be food for a hungry world. Whereas Caesar—in the manner of Eve and Adam—existed to be fed, Jesus existed to be fed upon. He was destined to be, not only the host at the sacred banquet, but (how like Babette here) the meal itself. And to Christ's manger came the shepherds (evocative of the poor and marginalized, the lost sheep of the house of Israel) and kings (evocative of the nations of the world), drawn there as though by a magnet. Thus commenced the realization of Isaiah's vision. A story that can be found in all three of the synoptic Gospels is that of the conversion of Levi (or Matthew) the tax collector. We hear that as Jesus was passing by, he spotted Matthew at his tax collector's post. To be a tax collector in Jesus' time—a Jew

---

11. Raymond E. Brown, *The Birth of the Messiah* (Garden City, NY: Image Books, 1977), esp. 48ff. and 249ff.

collaborating with the Roman occupying power in the oppression of one's own people—was to be a contemptible figure, someone akin to a French collaborator during the Nazi period. Jesus gazed at this man and said, simply, "Follow me." Did Jesus invite Matthew because the tax collector merited it? Was Jesus responding to a request from Matthew or some hidden longing in the sinner's heart? Certainly not. Grace, by definition, comes unbidden and without explanation. In Caravaggio's magnificent painting of this scene, Matthew, dressed anachronistically in sixteenth-century finery, responds to Jesus' summons by pointing incredulously to himself and wearing a quizzical expression, as if to say, "Me? You want me?" The hand of Christ in Caravaggio's painting is adapted from the hand of Adam in Michelangelo's depiction of the creation of man on the Sistine Chapel ceiling. Just as creation is *ex nihilo* (out of nothing), so conversion is a new creation, a gracious remaking of a person from the nonbeing of his sin. Matthew, we are told, immediately got up and followed the Lord. But where did he follow him? To a banquet! "And as he sat at dinner in the house . . ." is the first thing we read after the declaration that Matthew followed him (Matt. 9:10). Before he calls Matthew to do anything, before he sends him on mission, Jesus invites Matthew to recline in easy fellowship around a festive table. Erasmo Leiva-Merikakis comments, "The deepest meaning of Christian discipleship is not to work for Jesus but to be with Jesus."[12] The former tax collector listens to the Word, laughs with him, breaks bread with him, and in this finds his true identity. Adam was the friend of Yahweh before becoming, through his own fear and pride, Yahweh's enemy. Now Jesus, Yahweh made flesh, seeks to reestablish this lost friendship with Adam's descendants.

The Gospel then tells us that many other sinners and tax collectors, inspired, we presume, by Matthew's example, "came and were sitting with [Jesus] and his disciples" (Matt. 9:10). This is but one example of

---

12. Erasmo Leiva-Merikakis, *Fire of Mercy, Heart of the Word: Meditations on the Gospel According to St. Matthew*, vol. 1 (San Francisco: Ignatius Press, 1996), 424.

how Jesus embodies the Isaian vision of all the nations of the world streaming to unity around Mt. Zion. Christ himself is the meeting of divinity and humanity, and hence he *is* the temple, the place of right worship. And thus it is around him that the nations will gather to be fed "rich food filled with marrow" and "well-aged wines" (Isa. 25:6). The same grace that summoned Matthew now, through Matthew, summons the rest, and a community of sinners-become-diners is formed. Naturally, this coming together stirs up the resentment of the Pharisees, who ask the disciples, "Why does your teacher eat with tax collectors and sinners?" (Matt. 9:11). In our dysfunction, having lost contact with the God through whom all are one, we tend to order ourselves in exclusive and domineering ways, determining the insiders precisely in contradistinction to the outsiders. But this is just the kind of phony, self-destructive community that Jesus has come to interrupt. And so he responds to this criticism: "Those who are well have no need of a physician, but those who are sick. . . . For I have come to call not the righteous but sinners" (Matt. 9:12, 13).

Here we find a theme that will be developed throughout the tradition—namely, the sacred meal as medicine for the sin-sick soul. In light of Jesus' observation, we can see that the inclusion of sinners is the very heart and raison d'être of the meal that he hosts.

The miracle of the feeding of the thousands with a few loaves and fishes must have haunted the imaginations of the early Christian communities, for accounts of it can be found in all four Gospels. These narratives are richly iconic presentations of the great theme of the sacred meal that we have been developing. In Luke's version, crowds began to gather around Jesus when they heard that he had retired to Bethsaida. Moved with pity, Jesus taught them and cured their sick, but as the day was drawing to a close, the disciples worried about what this enormous crowd would eat. "The twelve came to him and said, 'Send the crowd away, so that they may go into the surrounding villages and countryside, to lodge and get provisions; for we are here in a deserted place'" (Luke 9:12). The Twelve, symbolic of the gathered tribes of Israel, act here in contradiction to their own deepest identity, for they want to scatter those whom Jesus has drawn magnetically to himself. So Jesus challenges them: "You give them something to eat." But they protest: "We have no more than five loaves and two fish—unless we are to go and buy food for all these people" (Luke 9:13). Oblivious to their complaint, Jesus instructs them to gather the crowd in groups of fifty or so. Then, taking the loaves and fish, Jesus said a blessing over them, broke them, and then gave them to the disciples for distribution. Everyone in the crowd of five thousand ate until they were satisfied.

There is no better exemplification in the Scriptures of what I have been calling the loop of grace. God offers, as a sheer grace, the gift of being, but if we try to cling to that gift and make it our own (in the manner of Eve and Adam), we lose it. The constant command of the Bible is this: what you have received as a gift, give as a gift—and you will find the original gift multiplied and enhanced. God's grace, precisely because it is *grace,* cannot be held on to; rather, it is had only in the measure that it remains grace—that is to say, a gift given away. God's life, in a word, is had only on the fly. One realizes this truth when one enters willingly into the loop of grace, giving away that which one is receiving. The hungry people who gather around Jesus in this scene are symbolic of the hungry human race, starving from the time of Adam and Eve for what will satisfy. In imitation of our first parents, we have tried to fill up the emptiness with wealth, pleasure, power, honor, the sheer love of domination, but none of it works, precisely because we have all been wired for God and God *is* nothing but love. It is only when we conform ourselves to the way of love, only when, in a high paradox, we contrive to empty out the ego, that we are filled. Thus the five loaves and two fish symbolize that which has been given to us, all that we have received as a grace from God. If we appropriate it, we lose it. But if we turn it over to Christ, then we will find it transfigured and multiplied, even unto the feeding of the world. At the outset of the story, the disciples refused to serve the crowd, preferring to send them away to the neighboring towns to fend for themselves. At the climax of the narrative, the disciples become themselves the instruments of nourishment, setting the loaves and fishes before the people. Within the loop of grace, they discovered their mission and were, themselves, enhanced, transfigured. The little detail at the end of the story—that the leftovers filled twelve wicker baskets—has an eschatological overtone. We are meant to think, once more, of Isaiah's holy mountain to which the twelve tribes of Israel and, through them, all the tribes of the world would be drawn.

All of these themes are summed up, drawn together, recapitulated (if I may use St. Irenaeus' language[13]) in the meal that Jesus hosted the night before his death. Luke tells us that, at the climactic moment of his life and ministry, Jesus "took his place at the table, and the apostles with him" (Luke 22:14). At this Last Supper, Jesus, in a culminating way, embodied Yahweh's desire to sit in easy intimacy with his people, sharing his life with them. He said, "I have eagerly desired to eat this Passover with you before I suffer" (Luke 22:15). As we saw, Yahweh established the Passover meal as a sign of his covenant with his holy people Israel. Thus Jesus, Yahweh made flesh, gathered his community around the Passover table. All of the familiar Passover motifs of liberation, redemption, unity, and festivity are at play here, but they are being redefined and reconfigured in relation to Jesus. The Isaian vision of the sumptuous meal on God's holy mountain is described as "eschatological," implying that it has to do with God's deepest and final desire for the world that he has made. At the commencement of the Last Supper, as he settled in with his disciples, Jesus explicitly evoked this eschatological dimension: "For I tell you, I will not eat it until it is fulfilled in the kingdom of God" (Luke 22:16). And when he took the first cup of Passover wine, he reiterated the theme: "For I tell you that from now on I will not drink of the fruit of the vine until

---

13. Irenaeus, *Against Heresies* 5.21.1 (*ANF* 1:548–549).

the kingdom of God comes" (Luke 22:18). It is most important to remember that this meal took place on the night before Jesus' death—which is to say, at the moment when he was summing up his life and preparing for his own Passover into the realm of the Father. Therefore, insisting that he will not eat or drink again until the kingdom arrives is tantamount to explaining that this meal has a final and unsurpassable symbolic significance, that it is his last word spoken, as it were, in the shadow of the eternal and thus redolent of the divine order. The room of the Last Supper *is* Isaiah's holy mountain, and the meal that Jesus hosts *is* the supper of rich food and well-aged wines. It is as though the longed-for future has appeared even now in time. What stood at the heart of this event? Jesus took the unleavened bread of the Passover, the bread symbolic of Israel's hasty flight from slavery to freedom, blessed it in accord with the traditional Passover prayer of blessing, broke it, and distributed it to his disciples saying, "This is my body, which is given for you. Do this in remembrance of me" (Luke 22:19). And then, after they had eaten, he took a cup of wine—traditionally called the cup of blessing—and said, "This cup that is poured out for you is the new covenant in my blood" (Luke 22:20). Acting once more in the very person of Yahweh, Jesus fed his friends with his very substance, effecting the deepest kind of coinherence *among* them because of the radicality of his own coinherence *with* them. To say "body" and "blood," in the nondualist context of first-century Judaism, is to say "self," and thus Jesus was inviting his disciples to feed on him and thereby to draw his life into theirs, conforming themselves to him in the most intimate and complete way possible. We must never keep the account of the fall far from our minds when we consider these events. If our trouble began with a bad meal (seizing at godliness on our own terms), then our salvation commences with a rightly structured meal (God offering us his life as a free gift). What was foreshadowed when Mary laid the Christ child in the manger came, at this meal, to full expression.

It is of great moment that, immediately after this extraordinary event—this constitution of the Church around God's gift of self—Jesus speaks of treachery: "But see, the one who betrays me is with me, and his hand is on the table" (Luke 22:21). In the biblical reading, God's desires have been, from the beginning, opposed. Consistently, human beings have preferred the isolation and separation of sin to the festivity of the sacred meal. Theologians have called this anomalous tendency the *mysterium iniquitatis* (the mystery of evil), for there is no rational ground for it, no reason why it should exist. But there it stubbornly is, always shadowing the good, parasitic upon that which it tries to destroy. Therefore, we should not be too surprised that, as the sacred meal comes to its richest possible expression, evil accompanies it. Judas the betrayer expresses the *mysterium iniquitatis* with particular symbolic power, for he had spent years in intimacy with Jesus, taking in the Lord's moves and thoughts at close quarters, sharing the table of fellowship with him, and yet he saw fit to turn Jesus over to his enemies and to interrupt the coinherence of the Last Supper. Those of us who regularly gather around the table of intimacy with Christ and yet engage consistently in the works of darkness are meant to see ourselves in the betrayer.

What follows is a scene that, were it not so tragic, would be funny. Having experienced at firsthand the intense act of love by which Jesus formed a new humanity around the eating of his Body and the drinking of his Blood, having sensed that the deepest meaning of this new life is self-sacrificing love, the disciples quarrel about titles and honors: "A dispute also arose among them as to which one of them was to be regarded as the greatest" (Luke 22:24). In the table fellowship that he practiced throughout his ministry, Jesus, as we saw, consistently undermined the systems of domination and the social stratifications that marked the culture of his time. His order (God's kingdom) would be characterized by an equality and mutuality born of our shared relationship to the creator God, who "makes his sun to shine on the evil and on the good" (Matt. 5:45). Therefore, games of ambition and claims of social superiority are inimical to the community that finds its point of orientation around the table of Jesus' Body and Blood. And this is why Jesus responded so promptly and unambiguously to the disciples' childish preoccupations: "The kings of the Gentiles lord it over them; and those in authority over them are called benefactors. But not so with you; rather the greatest among you must become like the youngest, and the leader like one who serves" (Luke 22:25–26).

If, as Feuerbach said, we are what we eat, then those who eat the Flesh of Jesus and drink his Blood must constitute a new society, grounded in love, service, nonviolence, and nondomination. Reminding them of their crucial importance as the first members of the Church, Jesus said, "I confer on you, just as my Father has conferred on me, a kingdom. . . . And you will sit on thrones judging the twelve tribes of Israel" (Luke 22:29–30). The order of love that obtains within God became flesh in Jesus and, through Jesus, was given to the community that he founded. That community in turn, the new Israel, would be, in accord with Isaiah's prediction, the means by which the whole world would be gathered to God. Here, the story of the multiplication of the loaves and fishes comes to mind. Initially, as we saw, the disciples refused their mission to be the new Israel and feed the crowd, but then, in light of the miracle of grace, they became the distributors of grace. A very similar dynamic is on display in the account of the Last Supper. It is never enough simply to eat and drink the Body and Blood of Jesus; one must become a bearer of the power that one has received. The meal always conduces to the mission.

The Last Supper preceded and symbolically anticipated the terrible events of the following day, when Jesus' body would indeed be given away and his blood poured out. In the next section of the book, I will speak much more of this sacrificial dimension of the supper, but for now I would like to focus on what followed the dying of Jesus. If Jesus had died and simply remained in his grave, he would be remembered (if he was remembered at all) as a noble idealist, tragically crushed by the forces of history. Perhaps a few of his disciples would have carried on his program for a time, but eventually the Jesus movement, like so many others like it, would have run out of steam. N.T. Wright, echoing the opinion of the Church Fathers, argued that the single most extraordinary fact of early Christianity is the perdurance of the Christian Church as a messianic movement. There could have been, in the first century, no surer sign that someone was *not* the Messiah than his death at the hands of the enemies of Israel, for one of the central marks of Messiahship was precisely victory over those enemies. That Peter, James, John, Paul, Thomas, and the rest could announce throughout the Mediterranean world that Jesus was in fact the long-awaited Israelite Messiah and that they could go to their deaths defending this claim are the surest indications that something monumentally significant happened to Jesus after his death. That something was the Resurrection. Though too many modern theologians have tried to explain the Resurrection away as a wish-fulfilling fantasy, a vague symbol, or a literary invention, the New Testament writers could not be clearer: the crucified Jesus, who had died and been buried, appeared alive again to his disciples.

The risen Christ was—as all of the accounts attest—strange. On the one hand, he was the same Jesus with whom they had eaten and drunk and to whom they had listened, but on the other hand, he was different, in fact so changed that frequently they didn't immediately recognize him or acknowledge him. It was as though he stood on the borderline between two worlds, still existing in this dimension of space and time, but also transcending it, participating in a higher, better world. Through certain hints in the Old Testament, some first-century Jews had begun to cultivate the conviction that at the end of time God would bring the righteous dead back to life and restore them to a transfigured earth. In the risen Jesus, the first Christians saw this hope being realized. In Paul's language, Christ was "the first fruits" of those who had fallen asleep—that is to say, the initial instance of the general resurrection of the dead. In him, they saw the dawn of the promised restoration. And thus they began to see that the sacred banquet was not simply an expression of full-flourishing in this world, not simply about justice, peace, and nonviolence here below, but also the anticipation of an elevated, transfigured, and perfected world where God's will would be completely done and his kingdom completely come.

One of the most beautiful evocations of this heavenly meal is found in the twenty-first chapter of John's Gospel. The author of John's Gospel was a literary genius, and his work is marked by subtle and intricate symbolism. Therefore, we must proceed carefully as we examine this story. He tells us that the risen Christ appeared to his disciples by the Sea of Tiberias in Galilee. Throughout the Gospels, beautiful Galilee, Jesus' home country, is symbolic of the land of resurrection and new life. After the Paschal events in Jerusalem, the disciples of Jesus had returned there and taken up, it appears, their old livelihood, for John tells us that seven of them, under the leadership of Peter, were in a boat heading out to fish. But we must attend to the mystical depth of the narrative. When he appeared to them after his Resurrection, Jesus, according to John, breathed on these disciples and said, "Receive the Holy Spirit" and "as the Father has sent me, so I send you" (John 20:21–22). Therefore, we should appreciate this fishing expedition as a symbol of the Church (the barque of Peter), across space and time, at its apostolic task of seeking souls. At the break of dawn, they spied a mysterious figure on the distant shore, who shouted out to them, "Children, you have no fish, have you?" (John 21:5). When they answered in the negative, he instructed them to cast the net over the right side of the ship. When they did so, they brought in a huge catch of fish. The life and work of the Church, John seems to be telling us, will be a lengthy, twilight struggle, a hard toil that will often seem to bear little or no fruit. But after the long night, the dawn of a new life and a new order will break, the transfigured world inaugurated by Jesus. The catch of fish that he makes possible is the totality of people that Christ will gather to himself; it is the new Israel, the eschatological Church. We know this through a subtle bit of symbolism. When the fish are dragged ashore, John bothers to tell us their exact number, 153, a figure commonly taken in the ancient world to signify the total number of species of fish in the sea.

After the miraculous haul, the "disciple whom Jesus loved," traditionally identified as the author of the Gospel, shouted, "It is the Lord!" (John 21:7). St. John, the one who rested on the breast of the Lord at the Last Supper and who had the greatest intuitive feel for Jesus' intentions, represents here the mystical dimension of the Church. Up and down the centuries, there have been poets, preachers, teachers, liturgists, mystics, and saints who have an instinct for who Jesus is and what he desires. They are the ones who, typically, see the working of the Lord first, who recognize his purposes even before the leadership of the Church does. John's cry in this story anticipates their intuitions and discoveries. What the mystics and poets are ultimately sensing is the eschatological purpose of the Church, the shore toward which the barque of the Church is sailing. When Peter hears that it is the Lord, he throws on clothes. What seems like an incidental detail is symbolically rich. After their sin, Eve and Adam made clothes for themselves, for they were ashamed. So Peter, who had three times denied Jesus, felt similarly ashamed to appear naked before the Lord. He therefore represents, in this symbolic narrative, all those sinners across the centuries who will, in their shame and penitence, seek forgiveness from Christ. As the disciples come ashore, they see that Jesus is doing something altogether in character: he is hosting a meal for them. "They saw a charcoal fire there, with fish on it, and bread. . . . Jesus said to them, 'Come, have breakfast'" (John 21:9, 12). Symbolically, they have arrived at the end of time and the end of their earthly mission, and they are, at the dawn of a new age, ushered into the definitive banquet of which the meals from Eden through the Last Supper were but anticipations. Disciples, mystics, saints, and forgiven sinners are welcome at this breakfast inaugurating the new and elevated manner of being that God had wanted to give us from the time of the Garden of Eden.

The Eucharistic Liturgy

This entire story that I've sketched—creation, the fall, the formation of Israel, the Passover to freedom, the vision of Isaiah's holy mountain, the gracious table fellowship of Jesus, the Last Supper, and the eschatological banquet—is made present to us at the Mass. The Eucharistic liturgy of the Church sums up and reexpresses the history of salvation, culminating in the meal by which Jesus feeds us with his very self. What I would like to do in the remaining pages of this section is to walk through the Mass with this complex motif of the sacred meal in mind, demonstrating how the various features and elements we have explored are on vivid display in the liturgy.

Yahweh formed the people Israel as the means by which the whole of creation, wrecked by the fall, would be healed. The Passover supper was, as we saw, the symbolic expression of this communion so desired by God, the Isaiah mountain its eschatological anticipation, and Jesus' meals its concrete embodiment. The opening move of the Eucharistic liturgy takes place before the ritual proper commences, when people from all walks of life, varying educational backgrounds, different economic classes, of all ages and of both genders gather in one place to pray. In principle, there is no block or obstacle to those who wish to come to the Mass. When she was considering the possibility of becoming a Roman Catholic, Dorothy Day commented that what impressed her the most about the Mass was that the rich and the poor knelt there side by side in prayer.[14] A community that would never exist in the harsh

14. Dorothy Day, *From Union Square to Rome* (Silver Spring, MD: Preservation of the Faith, 1938), 15.

world of 1930s America strangely existed around the altar of Christ, God's desire for the world becoming incarnate even in the midst of sin. When the great English historian Christopher Dawson informed his aristocratic mother that he was converting from Anglicanism to Catholicism, she objected, not to his shift in doctrinal affiliation, but that he would be obliged, in her words, to "worship with the help." The gathered community, coming together to worship the Lord and to feed on him, is indeed the seed of a new way of being, the contravention of the divisions and hatreds that flowed from the fall. It is the new world emerging within the very structure of the old.

Once assembled, the community rises to sing. Liturgical music ought not to be seen as secondary or merely decorative, for it gives expression to the harmonizing of the many. Just as the tribes that stream up the holy mountain do not lose their individuality as they gather to worship in common, so the participants at Mass do not surrender their distinctiveness when they sing together. Rather, they contribute, individually, to a consonance. Just after the sign of the cross and the greeting, the people are invited to acknowledge their sin and seek the divine mercy; they say, "Kyrie eleison; Christe eleison; Kyrie eleison" (Lord, have mercy; Christ, have mercy; Lord, have mercy).[15] Jesus came, not for the healthy, but for the sick. He was Yahweh in person calling home the scattered sheep of the house of Israel, and that is why he was so gracious in his welcome to Matthew and his disreputable friends. And so we sinners (once we accept that we are indeed sinners) are forgiven and welcomed into easy intimacy with Christ at the liturgy. At Sunday Mass and at more festive Masses, the Kyrie is followed by the great prayer of the Gloria, which begins with this line: "Glory to God in the highest, and on earth peace to people of good will."[16] Much of the theology that we've been presenting is packed into that statement. Peace will break out on earth, in accord with God's first and

---

15. *Roman Missal.*
16. *Roman Missal.*

deepest desire, when we all come together in a common act of worship. Aristotle remarked that a friendship will never last as long as the friends are simply in love with one another. In time, he said, such a relationship will devolve into mutual egotism. Rather, a friendship will endure only in the measure that the two friends fall together in love with a transcendent third, with some great value or good that lies beyond the grasp of either of them.[17] This Aristotelian principle applies in regard to our relationship with God. The indispensable key to peace—that is to say, a flourishing friendship among the members of the human race—is that we all fall together in love with the transcendent Creator. Only when we give glory to God in the highest—above nation, family, culture, political party, etc.—will we, paradoxically, find unity among ourselves. To put this in more explicitly scriptural language, only when we sit together at the meal hosted and made possible by God will we truly sit together in peace.

After the Gloria prayer, participants in the Mass are seated for the proclamation of the Word of God. Since Christ is, as St. John insisted, the Word of God made flesh, the entire Scripture—Old Testament and New—is the speech of Christ. Having been gathered by Jesus, we listen to him, as did the crowds who heard the Sermon on the Mount. In the ancient world, the meal, at which convivial friends reclined in easy company, was the place where philosophical conversation often took place. (Think of the *Symposium* of Plato, an account of a festive supper during which the conversants discoursed on the nature of love). Thus, just as Jesus taught people around the table of conversation and good cheer, so he teaches us who have gathered in fellowship for the Eucharistic liturgy.

The second major section of Mass—the Liturgy of the Eucharist—commences with the offertory presentation. From the midst of the congregation, simple gifts of bread, wine, and water are brought forward and placed on the altar. Here we have a quite exact symbolic

17. Aristotle, *Nicomachean Ethics* 8.

re-presentation of the multiplication of the loaves and fishes. The priest, who is acting in the person of Christ, sees the crowd gathered before him and wonders how he might feed them spiritually. From the people, he garners a small amount of food and drink, which he then presents to the Father: "Blessed are you, Lord God of all creation, for through your goodness we have received the bread and wine we offer you."[18] Because the Creator God stands in need of nothing, he is able to receive these gifts and send them back elevated and multiplied, transformed into the Body and Blood of Jesus. Our small offerings, in short, break against the rock of the divine self-sufficiency and return to us as spiritual food and drink. The Mass, accordingly, is the richest possible expression of the loop of grace, God's life possessed in the measure that it is given away.

At this point, I would like to say a word about the cosmic dimension of the Mass. As we have seen, sin is construed, in the biblical reading, as not simply a personal and interpersonal problem, a strictly human concern. Rather, sin compromises the integrity of the entire created order. Thus, the salvation wrought through Israel and Jesus and made present in the Mass has to do with the healing of the world. We see this dimension especially in the gifts of bread and wine presented at the offertory. To speak of bread is to speak, implicitly, of soil, seed, grain, and sunshine that crossed ninety million miles of space; to speak of wine is to speak, indirectly, of vine, earth, nutrients, storm clouds, and rainwater. To mention earth and sun is to allude to the solar system of which they are a part, and to invoke the solar system is to assume the galaxy of which it is a portion, and to refer to the galaxy is to hint at the unfathomable realities that condition the structure of the measurable universe. Therefore, when these gifts are brought forward, it is as though the whole of creation is placed on the altar before the Lord. In the older Tridentine liturgy, the priest would make this presentation facing the

---

18. *Roman Missal.*

east, the direction of the rising sun, signaling that the Church's prayer was on behalf not simply of the people gathered in that place but of the cosmos itself.

Next, through the power of the words of the Eucharistic Prayer, the elements of bread and wine are transfigured into the Body and Blood of Jesus, and the people are invited to come forward and feast on the Lord. This, once again, is the Christ of the Bethlehem manger, offered for the sustenance of the world. The participants in the Mass don't simply listen to the teaching of Jesus; they don't merely call his memory and spirit to mind. They eat and drink him, incorporating him into themselves, or better, becoming incorporated into him. An element of Catholic ecclesiology that modern Americans find especially difficult to comprehend is that the Church is not a collectivity of like-minded individuals, something akin to the Abraham Lincoln Society or the Chamber of Commerce. In accord with St. Paul's master image, the Church is a Body, a living organism composed of interdependent cells, molecules, and organs. Christ Jesus is the Head of this Body, and its lifeblood is his sacramental grace, especially the grace of the Eucharist. The members of the Church, those who consume his Body and Blood, become therefore the limbs, eyes, ears, and sensibilities of Christ's Body, the means by which his work continues in the world. Furthermore, they come to be connected to one another by an organic bond that goes dramatically beyond the cohesiveness of even the most intense of voluntary societies. Just as the stomach (if I can extrapolate a bit from Paul) could not possibly remain indifferent to a cancer growing in an adjacent organ, so one member of the Body of Christ couldn't possibly ignore the spiritual plight or physical need of another. And *all* people, Thomas Aquinas taught, are either explicitly or implicitly members of Christ's Body.[19] The radicality of Catholic social commitment—a concern for any and all who suffer—follows directly from the radicality of this distinctive ecclesiology.

19. Thomas Aquinas, *Summa theologiae* 3.8.3 ad 1.

Now, the Mass does not conclude with the reception of the Eucharist; it concludes rather with a commission: "Go forth, the Mass is ended."[20] It has been said that, after the words of consecration, those words of dismissal are the most sacred in the liturgy. We must recall, once more, that the community gathered around Jesus, descended from the twelve Apostles, is the new Israel and that the purpose of Israel was to be a beacon for the nations, the magnetic point to which all peoples would be drawn. Therefore, once filled with the Body and Blood of the Lord, galvanized as a new community formed according to the purposes of God, the people must go forth to Christify the world. Just as Noah released the life that he had preserved on the ark, so the priest sends the community out as the seed of new life. It is in this mission to feed a hungry world that we see the real point and purpose of the sacred meal.

We saw that the sacred meal is not limited in meaning and scope to this context of space and time alone; rather, it is situated within a properly eschatological framework. The Mass signals this transcendent dimension in a number of ways. In the Confiteor, the liturgy invokes another world: "I ask blessed Mary ever-Virgin, all the Angels and Saints, and you, my brothers and sisters, to pray for me to the Lord our God,"[21] and the great Gloria prayer calls to mind the song of the angels early on Christmas morning: "Glory to God in the highest heaven, and on earth peace among those whom he favors" (Luke 2:14). From the beginning of the rite, therefore, we are situated in a properly heavenly context that stretches beyond that of the community gathered immediately around us. We are praying to and with the heavenly court, composed of glorified human saints and spiritual creatures at a qualitatively higher pitch of existence. Furthermore, between the preface and the commencement of the Eucharistic Prayer proper, we find this distinctive prayer: "Holy,

---

20. *Roman Missal.*
21. *Roman Missal.*

43

Holy, Holy, Lord God of hosts. Heaven and earth are full of your glory, hosanna in the highest."[22] The triple holy mimics precisely the cry of the angels in a scene from the sixth chapter of the book of the prophet Isaiah. As the prophet saw a vision of God, he heard attendants at the heavenly throne invoking the creator of the universe with this triple chant. The Christian tradition has, naturally enough, taken these three angelic "holies" to designate the three persons of the Blessed Trinity. The point is that as the worshiping community enters into the most sacred part of the Mass, it becomes conscious, once again, of the supernatural community that worships in tandem with it.

In his treatment of the Eucharist in the *Summa theologiae,* Thomas Aquinas said that the sacrament has three names, each one corresponding to one of the dimensions of time. As we look to the past, we call the sacrament *sacrificium* (sacrifice), for it embodies the self-immolation of Christ on the cross. About this feature we will have much more to say in the next section. But secondly, as we look to the present, we call it *communio* (communion), since it realizes the coming together of the body of Christ here and now. Finally, as we look to the future, we call it *Eucharistia* (Eucharist), since it antici-pates the great thanksgiving that will take place in heaven when we are in the company of the holy ones, at the eschatological banquet.[23] It is this final feature that the liturgy emphasizes when it invokes so consistently the angels and saints.

Conclusion

God is, in his ownmost reality, not a monolith, but a communion of persons. From all eternity, the Father speaks himself, and this Word that he utters *is* the Son. A perfect image of his Father, the Son shares

22. *Roman Missal.*
23. Thomas Aquinas, *Summa theologiae* 3.73.4.

fully the actuality of the Father: unity, omniscience, omnipresence, spiritual power. This means that, as the Father gazes at the Son, the Son gazes back at the Father. Since each is utterly beautiful, the Father falls in love with the Son and the Son with the Father—and they sigh forth their mutual love. This holy breath (*Spiritus Sanctus*) *is* the Holy Spirit. These three "persons" are distinct, yet they do not constitute three Gods. They are the way the one God is constituted in the depth of his own being. This means that, for Christian faith, God *is* a family of love, a sharing of life, a breathing in and breathing out, a looking toward another. Whereas for the ancient philosophers substance is ontologically superior to relationship, for Christian theology relationship is metaphysically basic, for God *is* nothing but love. The whole history of salvation can be read as the Trinitarian God's attempt to draw the human family into a relationship that mimics the love that God is. When we love God with our whole heart and mind, we necessarily love all those whom God has loved into existence.

This family love is expressed in the great biblical image of the sacred banquet that we have been exploring throughout this chapter. The Eucharist sums it up and brings it to perfect expression, and hence the Eucharist is the richest participation in the very being of the God who is nothing but love.

Chapter 2

THE EUCHARIST
AS SACRIFICE

We recall that the joy, festivity, and spiritual power of Babette's feast were made possible by an extraordinary sacrifice, acted out for the most part quietly and off-stage. Only when the sisters saw Babette, pale and exhausted, sitting on the butcher's block and heard her tale of self-emptying love, did they realize the price that was paid for their *sacrum convivium,* their holy banquet. This feature of Dinesen's story bespeaks an elemental biblical truth: in a world gone wrong, there is no communion without sacrifice. Since the world has been twisted out of shape, it can be straightened only through a painful process of reconfiguration. It is practically impossible to read any two pages of the Bible in succession without coming across the language of God's anger, but we mustn't interpret this symbolic expression literally, as though God passes in and out of emotional snits. The divine wrath is a theological symbol for the justice of God—which is to say, God's passion to set things right. In his love, God cannot allow his fallen world to remain in alienation; rather, he must do the hard work of drawing it back into communion. And this means that God is continually about the business of sacrifice.

In the years following Vatican II, the meal dimension of the Eucharist was almost exclusively emphasized, both by theologians and by pastoral practitioners. The active participation of the community, gathered at the banquet of the Lord, was given pride of place. The classical description of the Mass as a sacrifice was muted, and the locale where the priest celebrated the sacrament was referred to for the most part as a "table" and not as an "altar." This shift of focus was undoubtedly an attempt to correct an excessive stress on the sacrificial dimension of the Eucharist prior to the council, but the pendular swing did not help the Church. When the two aspects of the Eucharist—meal and sacrifice—are separated, the biblical principle that I articulated above is compromised, and the Mass can devolve into something less than fully serious. There can be no communion without sacrifice, and thus there is no Eucharistic table that is not, at the same time, an altar. In this second section, I would like to explore the sacrificial dimension of the Eucharist, and as I did in the previous section, I would like to conduct my analysis within a wide biblical framework.

Sacrifice in the Old Testament

In the last chapter, we saw how the author of Genesis articulated the fundamental problem as self-deification, the all-too-human tendency to cling to godliness rather than to surrender to God. This spiritual disorder conduced to a rapid disintegration of the coinherence that God wanted to hold sway in his creation. In the wake of the original rupture with God, man was pitted against woman and woman against man—and both were pitted against nature, love having been replaced by suspicion and violence. The consequence, in Yeats' poetic language: "The center cannot hold . . . and mere anarchy is loosed upon the world."[1] The Bible recounts this moral and spiritual declension with its typical narrative laconicism. Cain and Abel, the sons of Adam and Eve, fell out of friendship, and Cain ruthlessly slew his brother, becoming, in a telling detail, the founder of cities. (Is there, in the literature of

---

1. W.B. Yeats, "The Second Coming," in *The Major Works*, ed. Edward Larrissy (Oxford: Oxford University Press, 1997), 91.

the world, any more devastating critique of the way human beings tend to organize themselves?) By the time of Noah, "the wickedness of humankind was great in the earth, and . . . every inclination of the thoughts of their hearts was only evil continually" (Gen. 6:5), and God accordingly sent a great flood to wipe out life on the earth.

Often in the biblical stories, flood waters are evocative of the primal, watery chaos that held sway before God brought forth the order of creation. Hence they are expressive, not of God's arbitrary punishment, but of the destructive power of sin. After Noah, the human race became once more a dysfunctional family. Chapter 11 of Genesis tells us that the whole earth had only one language and that the people joined together in a great project to build a city at the center of which would be a tower reaching up to challenge the heavens (Gen. 11:1–4). This Tower of Babel functions as a neat biblical image of the aggressive, self-aggrandizing, and imperialistic tendencies of human beings once they have lost contact with God. We ought not to read these Genesis tales, of course, as straightforward history, but rather as densely textured symbolic narratives that express, with admirable economy, the fundamental features and aspects of sin: violence, arrogance, division, blaming, deception, lust for power, and murder. However, as we saw in the last chapter, the God of justice will not rest. In the scriptural reading, he sets himself the task of saving his compromised creation, and the principal means that he chooses is the formation of a people who would learn to walk in his ways and would become thereby a light to all the nations. Just after the story of the Tower of Babel there commences the great narrative concerning Abram of Ur, the father of the nation of Israel. The first thing we hear about Abram is that he is called by the Lord: "Now the Lord said to Abram, 'Go from your country and your kindred and your father's house to the land that I will show you. I will make of you a great nation'" (Gen. 12:1–2). The essential problem began with disobedience, and thus the solution must begin with obedience. Eve and Adam became rebels; Abram must, accordingly, become a servant. He is being told to uproot his entire life and to move, with his family, to a distant land he knows nothing about—and he is, we are informed, seventy-five years old. To cling to godliness, in the manner of our first parents, is to claim lordship over one's own life; to surrender to God is to realize that one's life is not one's own, that a higher and more compelling voice commands. In all of this, we sense that friendship with God (a covenant with him) would involve sacrifice, the abandonment of the self, and we begin to see the spiritual importance of this juxtaposition, for God's promise to Abram involves what I've been calling the loop of grace. If Abram can contrive a way to make of his life a gift—if he can sacrifice in trust what God has given to him—then his being will increase: "I will make of you a great nation." As Abram, in faith, sets out with his family, the long pedagogy begins. The rest of the biblical narrative, up to and including the story of Jesus, is the account of God's formation of the clan of Abram, a people after his own heart, and this education will center around the intertwined themes of covenant and sacrifice. In chapter 15 of Genesis, Abram hears, once again, the divine promise that he will become a great nation, his descendants more numerous than the stars of the sky, but then he, reasonably enough, complains, "O LORD God, what will you give me, for I continue childless?" (Gen. 15:2). In answer, God gives a series of peculiar commands: "Bring me a heifer three years old, a female goat three years old, a ram three years old, a turtledove, and a young pigeon" (Gen. 15:9). He then instructs Abram to cut these animals in two and place them down. As it grew dark, Abram fell into a kind of trance, and "a smoking fire pot and a flaming torch passed between these pieces" (Gen. 15:17). On that day, Genesis tells us, God made a covenant (*Berith*) with Abram, saying, "To your descendants I give this land" (Gen. 15:18). I realize how odd, even incomprehensible, all of this can seem to us. Why should the establishment of a covenant between divinity and humanity be accompanied by a bizarre twilight ceremony involving butchered animals?

In order to grasp the matter, we have to abandon our perhaps overly tidy and antiseptic view of God and enter into the far earthier, more elemental world of the biblical imagination. Ancient peoples—Babylonians, Assyrians, Greeks, Romans, Celts, Aztecs, and Hebrews—came together in the practice of offering sacrifice to God or the gods. The idea, in itself, is relatively simple, though it was expressed in a wide variety of ceremonies and practices. Some part of the earth is returned to the divine principle—offered up—in order to establish communion with the sacred power. In the Hebrew context, both grain and animals were sacrificed to God, either as thank-offerings, sin-offerings, or simply as signals of communion and fellowship. But in even the most benign of sacrifices, some living thing was destroyed. According to the scholars of Hebrew religious practice, the destruction of grain or animal was meant to signal the sacrificer's offering and rending of himself. The offerer says, in effect, that what is happening to this animal—as in the case of the Abramic sacrifice we have been considering—should happen to me if I fall out of friendship with God; or, as this animal's lifeblood is poured out, so I symbolically pour out my own life in devotion and thanksgiving.

And thus we can appreciate the link between sacrifice and covenant. When God makes his *Berith* (covenant) with Abram, he is claiming Abram as totally his. ("I will be your God, and you will be my people," becomes a stock characterization of the terms of the covenants that God makes with Israel up and down the centuries). Scott Hahn, who has made a careful study of covenant in the Bible, makes an important distinction between covenant and contract.[2] Though the two have certain features in common—most especially the delineation of mutual obligations—the signal difference is that a contract determines "*what* is mine" while a covenant determines "*who* is mine." But the covenant has to be sealed by a sacrifice because we live in a world that

---

2. Scott Hahn and John Bergsma, "Covenant," in *The Oxford Encyclopedia of the Bible and Theology*, vol. 1, ed. Samuel E. Balentine (Oxford: Oxford University Press, 2015), 151–166.

is off-kilter. Prior to the fall, the human pledge of fidelity to God would have been effortless, a sheer joy; but after the fall, it must come at a cost, and through a painful reconfiguration of the self. It is this inner sacrifice that is expressed symbolically through the exterior offering of grain or animal.

Nowhere is the awful link between covenant and sacrifice on clearer display than in the story recounted in the twenty-second chapter of Genesis: Abraham's binding of his son Isaac. Abram's name, we learn, had been changed to Abraham when God had, still again, promised that he would become the father of many nations. Though he remained childless well into extreme old age, Abraham continued to hope in God's promise. One day, three strangers appeared at Abraham's tent, and after the patriarch showed them hospitality, they promised that, upon their return the following year, Sarah, his wife, would be fondling a son. Though Sarah laughed upon hearing the prediction, Abraham trusted, and the prophecy came true. Isaac was thus not only the beloved child of Abraham's old age, but he was the fulfillment of God's covenant, the means by which God would raise up for him a mighty nation. Abraham's faith in Yahweh—his covenant with the Lord—was inextricably bound up with the existence of this son. And then, inexplicably and without warning, Yahweh demanded that Abraham offer his son in sacrifice: God said to him, "Abraham. . . . Take your son, your only son Isaac, whom you love, and go to the land of Moriah, and offer him there as a burnt offering" (Gen. 22:2). We saw that the relationship between Yahweh and Abraham began with a summons to trust and that Abraham's faith had deepened and broadened over time—but now his willingness to accept the word of God was being put to the ultimate test, precisely because this command of God seemed to place God in contradiction to himself. This order must have prompted within Abraham not only a personal, psychological crisis of the highest degree, but also, if I can express it this way, a theological crisis. In a supreme paradox, God wanted Abraham to ratify the covenant by a willingness to sacrifice the very condition for the possibility of the covenant. He was to surrender what was dearest to him, to give Isaac to God, seeing his son, not primarily as his own possession, but rather as God's gift and ingredient in God's mysterious design.

In the course of three terrible days, we are told, Abraham led Isaac to the mountain of sacrifice, enduring even the plaintive question of his son, "The fire and the wood are here, but where is the lamb for a burnt offering?" (Gen. 22:7). As the rabbis and commentators have made clear, Abraham must have gone through a spiritual and psychological torture beggaring description. Then, at the climactic moment, as he was about to plunge the knife into his son, an angel spoke, telling Abraham to desist: "Do not lay a hand on the boy or do anything to him; for now I know that you fear God, since you have not withheld your son, your only son, from me" (Gen. 22:12). We can see why this story of the *Aqedah* (binding) loomed so large in Israelite history, surpassing in spiritual significance even the events of Sinai. If, as we have been arguing, the basic human problem began with self-assertion to the point of self-deification, then the solution must come through the most radical kind of self-surrender to God, through that absolute trust that the Bible calls faith. Israel at its best—including that supreme Israelite, Jesus of Nazareth—will be conditioned by the power of Abraham's faith. And the covenant, union between God and humanity, will always be accompanied by a willingness to sacrifice.

The next great covenant that God makes with Israel is associated with Moses and the Exodus from Egypt. Like so many of the heroes of Israel, Moses had to be tested before he was ready for mission. This child of privilege, raised in the court of the pharaoh, was compelled to wander for many years in the desert, learning the humble ways of a shepherd, for God wanted him not to lord it over the people but to guide them and sacrifice for them. Only after this trial did Moses see the burning bush and hear the voice of God announcing the divine name, "I Am Who I Am" (Exod. 3:14). This divine title, so puzzling and abstract, is actually of salvific importance. As "the one who is," God is not one being among many, a local divinity who can be manipulated or avoided; rather, he is the Creator, the one who suffuses all things even as he radically transcends them. And this means that he can be neither grasped nor avoided, neither controlled nor ignored. Having encountered this God, in whose presence trust is the only proper response, Moses was ready for mission. And, as we've come to expect, this mission would involve self-surrender. God sent his servant back to Egypt, to the place where his people were enslaved, and he gave him the charge of leading the captives to freedom. He was to go into the heart of darkness, into the land of oppression, and through his own blood and sweat and obedience, to lead the Israelites back to liberty and right worship. Moses' dangerous confrontations with the pharaoh, as well as his patient endurance of his own people's complaints, were part of the liberator's sacrifice. On the eve of their escape, Moses told the people to gather in small groups and to prepare the Passover lamb. This sacred banquet was indeed, as we saw in the last chapter, the reenactment of humanity's long-lost intimacy with God, but we mustn't forget that it was made possible by the bloody sacrifice of an animal. For Israel, therefore, the Passover meal was to be a continual reminder of the price paid for freedom and communion.

Once escaped from oppression, the people, under Moses' leadership, came to Sinai, the mountain of the Lord, where they were given the two tablets of the Law. The Ten Commandments provided instruction for an interior renewal of the tribe. Through them, the children of Israel were (at least in principle) pulled back into shape, reformed as a people who love God above all things and who engage, consistently, in the works of compassion and justice. At their worst, they reacted (and continued to react) rather violently against these commands, seeing them as arbitrary external impositions. But God intended them as a sort of sacrifice, a painful but ultimately beneficial remaking of the sinful self. Now the interior sacrifice of the Law (the Torah) would be accompanied by an exterior sacrifice. Having declared the Law and heard the acquiescence of the people, Moses ordered the slaughter of oxen for the well-being of Israel, and then he "took half of the blood and put it in basins, and half of the blood he dashed against the altar," and the other half he "dashed . . . on the people and said, 'See the blood of the covenant that the LORD has made with you in accordance with these words'" (Exod. 24:6–8).

The idea behind this practice is straightforward enough: the splashing of the blood on the people signaled God's pledge of fidelity (his lifeblood) to them, and the splashing on the altar represented Israel's reciprocal pledge of fidelity to Yahweh, each saying to the other, in effect, "As this blood is poured out, so will my life be poured out for you." Once more the linking of covenant and sacrifice was on clear display. It is, incidentally, by no means accidental that this confluence of Torah and sacrifice precipitated the emergence of the formal Israelite priesthood. The book of Exodus details how Moses' brother Aaron and his sons were chosen as priests of Yahweh and charged with the task of worship and sacrifice. We hear of elaborate instructions for the construction of altars, the making of vestments, and the preparation of a whole array of liturgical accoutrements, all of it focused on the priestly (sacrificial) ministry.

The final great covenant that God "cut" (the typical biblical word) with Israel took place during the time of King David. After various types of tests—most notably his confrontation, armed only with slingshot and faith, with the giant Goliath, and his long battle with the jealous Saul—David emerged as a worthy shepherd of Israel. After David had brought the ark of the covenant into the city of Jerusalem, pledging thereby Israel's fidelity to Yahweh, the Lord spoke to the king through the prophet Nathan: "I will raise up your offspring after you . . . and I will establish his kingdom. Your house and your kingdom shall be made sure forever before me; your throne shall be established forever" (2 Sam. 7:12, 16). To Abraham, God had promised descendants more numerous than the stars in the sky, and to David, he promised a line of kingly successors, enduring, mysteriously enough, eternally. Both of these covenantal promises were expressions of the great biblical principle that self-donation leads to the increase of being, and they would be brought to fulfillment, in the Christian reading, through Christ and his Body the Church.

In light of what we've already seen, we shouldn't be surprised that this final covenant would also be accompanied by sacrifice. After the death of David, his immediate successor, Solomon, undertook the enormous project of building a temple to Yahweh in the holy city of Jerusalem. In that place, tied so closely to the Davidic line of kings, priests would for five centuries perform animal and grain sacrifice, and then when the temple was rebuilt after the return from the Babylonian exile, Israelite priests would carry on their sacrificial practice there until the second temple was destroyed by the Romans in AD 70. Thus, for nearly one thousand years, the Israelite nation ratified its covenant with Yahweh through the slaughter of beasts and the smoke of holocausts. They thereby massively demonstrated, in a symbolic manner, that the communion and life that Yahweh desired for his people would be made possible by an interior sacrifice, a pouring out of the self. The richest and most significant liturgical act in the temple took place every year on the Day of Atonement. The high priest would enter the Holy of Holies, the sanctuary at the very center of the temple complex, and there he would slaughter a goat, whose blood he would then sprinkle around the sacred place. Next, he would come out of the Holy of Holies, passing through the symbolic veil and sprinkling the remaining blood on the gathered crowd. He was, of course, reenacting the scene from Exodus that we analyzed above, signaling Israel's gift of its lifeblood to God and God's pledge of forgiveness to Israel. In his own person, he was acting as the mediator between divinity and humanity, a priest offering sacrifice on behalf of the people and, strangely enough, on behalf of

Yahweh himself. In the process, he was making symbolically real the restoration of creation according to God's intentions.

Now, though covenant and sacrifice were defining elements of ancient Israelite religion, though the Jewish people understood themselves in and through these central themes, there is, throughout the biblical period, a nagging sense that the covenant has never been truly fulfilled and sacrifice never completely efficacious. No matter how many times the covenant was taught, renewed, reaffirmed, it was broken by stubborn Israel, a "stiff-necked" people (Exod. 32:9). And no matter how many sacrifices were offered in the temple, Yahweh was still not properly honored and the people still not interiorly reformed. No one expresses this dissatisfaction better than the prophet Isaiah. Speaking the words of Yahweh, Isaiah says, "What to me is the multitude of your sacrifices? says the LORD; I have had enough of burnt offerings of rams and the fat of fed beasts; I do not delight in the blood of bulls, or of lambs, or of goats" (Isa. 1:11). Why would the God who demanded sacrifice now seem so indifferent, even hostile, to it? The answer comes: "Wash yourselves; make yourselves clean; remove the evil of your doings from before my eyes; cease to do evil, learn to do good; seek justice, rescue the oppressed, defend the orphan, plead for the widow" (Isa. 1:16 –17). What annoys Yahweh is not sacrifice in itself but sacrifice that has become divorced from the real work of compassion and justice, from the demands of the covenant. Such sacrifice has devolved into an empty symbol.

The prophet Jeremiah, who shares much of Isaiah's deep impatience with the corruption of the Israelite people and their rulers, nevertheless gives voice to a longing and a hope that must have been deeply planted in the collective consciousness of the nation. He expresses Yahweh's own pledge that he himself would one day fulfill the covenant and forgive the sins of the people. In the thirty-first chapter of the book of the prophet Jeremiah, we find these extraordinary words: "The days are surely coming, says the Lord, when I will make a new covenant with the house of Israel and the house of Judah. It will not be like the covenant I made with their ancestors . . . a covenant that they broke. . . . But this is the covenant that I will make with the house of Israel after those days. . . . I will put my law within them, and I will write it on their hearts; and I will be their God, and they shall be my people" (Jer. 31:31–33). All the prophets know that the covenants God has made with Israel—through Abraham, Moses, and David—have failed, due to the people's infidelity, but Jeremiah dreams that one day, through Yahweh's own direct intervention, a faithful Israel will emerge, a people who have a heart for the Lord, who consider the law not an external imposition, but a joy.

Let us take one more step. How will this renewal take place? How will Yahweh plant the law so deep in the children of Israel that their fulfillment of the covenant will be effortless? To find the answers, we must turn to some mysterious texts in the book of the prophet Isaiah, texts that particularly fascinated the first Christians. In the fifty-second chapter, we find a reference to a figure called the "servant" of the Lord, who, we are told, "shall be exalted and lifted up, and shall be very high" (Isa. 52:13). The nations of the earth will see him in this prominent position, but they shall not be looking at a splendid warrior or a majestic victor. Instead, they will be astonished at how "marred was his appearance, beyond human semblance" (Isa. 52:14). In chapter fifty-three, the description of this servant continues: "He had no form or majesty that we should look at him, nothing in his appearance that we should desire him. He was despised and rejected by others; a man of suffering and acquainted with infirmity" (Isa. 53:2–3). And then the reason for his deformation and anguish is made clearer: "Surely he has borne our infirmities and carried our diseases. . . . He was wounded for our transgressions, crushed for our iniquities. . . . And the Lord has laid on him the iniquity of us all" (Isa. 53:4–6). This "suffering servant" is presented, in short, as a sacrificial figure, one who will, on behalf of the entire nation, offer himself for the sins of the many. His greatness will consist, not in personal independence and political power, but rather in his willingness to bear the weight of sin, to disempower sin, as it were, from within. In a word, the covenant of which Jeremiah speaks (the writing of the law in the hearts of the people) would be effected through the sacrificial servant of whom Isaiah speaks. Having considered these many strains of Old Testament theology, and having seen the tight correlation between Jeremiah's everlasting covenant and Isaiah's suffering servant, we are ready, finally, to speak of Jesus and his sacrifice.

Jesus the Lamb of God

One of the earliest heresies that the Christian church fought was Marcionism, the conviction that Jesus should be interpreted in abstraction from the Old Testament. I spent so much time drawing together the Old Testament themes of covenant and sacrifice because I share the anti-Marcionite conviction that it is impossible to make sense of Jesus apart from his Jewishness. The categories that Paul and the Gospel writers used to present Jesus as the Christ were, almost exclusively, drawn from the Hebrew Scriptures. One reason that we have today such a difficult time appreciating Jesus is that we have become, effectively, Marcionite—that is to say, indifferent to, and/or ignorant of, the Bible. Without a properly Israelite preparation, most of the Christological language of the New Testament and the dogmatic tradition remains opaque.

For example, in the official teaching of the Church, formulated at the Council of Chalcedon in 451, Jesus is described as the coming together of two natures—divine and human—in the unity of the divine person. Though it can seem desperately abstract, this formula takes on density and resonance when we consider it against the backdrop of the Israelite theology of covenant that we sketched. As we saw, from Abraham through David, Yahweh pledged that he would be Israel's God and Israel would be his special people. However, despite God's fidelity, the covenant consistently came apart, due to the people's sin. What the first Christians discerned was that in Jesus the long-desired covenant was finally fulfilled, that divinity and humanity had indeed embraced, that God's will and the will of faithful Israel had fallen, at last, into harmony. And this is precisely what, in their more philosophically accented language, the fathers of the Council of Chalcedon were saying. And thus the Chalcedonian statement is but a more conceptually exact rendition of what John the Evangelist tells us in the prologue to his Gospel: "And the Word became flesh and lived among us" (John 1:14). The Word of God's covenantal love, which was addressed to Abraham, Moses, David, Isaiah, and Jeremiah, has now entered into a radical union with the flesh of this particular Israelite, Jesus from Nazareth, and thus, in this Jesus, the longing of Israel is fulfilled.

Now, covenant and sacrifice are always linked. Therefore when, in the Gospel of John, John the Baptist spies Jesus, he turns to a group of his disciples and says, "Look, here is the Lamb of God!" (John 1:36). This is one of the first and most important interpretive keys that John the Evangelist gives us: Jesus is the one who will play the role of the sacrificial lambs offered in the temple. In accord with our formula—no communion without sacrifice—Jesus, the covenant in person, will perforce be a sacrificed victim as well. Pope Leo the Great, writing in the sixth century, gave expression to a patristic commonplace when he said, "There was no other reason for the Son of God to be born than that he could be fixed to a cross."[3] Jesus came, in short, to be the suffering servant who would, through a sacrifice, take away the sins of the world. We find the same idea carved in stone on the façade of Chartres Cathedral. There isn't a trace of sentimentalism in the Chartres sculptor's depiction of the birth of Jesus: he shows Mary with a look of stoic acceptance and Jesus lying, not in a manger, but on a cold stone slab,

---

3. Leo the Great, "Sermon 48," in *St. Leo the Great: Sermons*, trans. Jane Patricia Freeland and Agnes Josephine Conway (Washington, DC: The Catholic University of America Press, 1996), 205.

the altar on which he would be offered. C.S. Lewis makes much the same point when he says that Jesus entered the world clandestinely and unobtrusively in the manner of a soldier sneaking behind enemy lines, for his mission would be the undermining of the fortress of sin.[4]

Let us look now at just a few Gospel scenes that are helpfully read under this rubric. Even the most skeptical of historical critics of the New Testament agree that Jesus was, at least in the earliest days of his ministry, connected to John the Baptist. Their confidence is based upon two criteria: multiple attestation (the Baptist is mentioned in all four Gospels) and embarrassment (elements that the Christian community would prefer to have suppressed but that still find their way into the Gospels are most likely based on historical fact). Why should the connection to John the Baptist be embarrassing to Jesus and the first Christians? Because John was offering a baptism of repentance and to him, consequently, sinners were flocking. One would suppose that the first Christian authors would have been a tad uneasy presenting the Savior of the world as someone who stood in need of a sinner's baptism. But this very tension provides, in fact, the best clue to reading this passage. Matthew tells us that Jesus "came from Galilee to John at the Jordan, to be baptized by him" (Matt. 3:13). Jesus did indeed slip into the muddy waters of the river and stand side by side with those seeking forgiveness, identifying himself with their condition. Anyone passing by would have presumed that Jesus was one sinner among many. When the Baptist saw him, he was taken aback: "John would have prevented him, saying, 'I need to be baptized by you, and do you come to me?'" (Matt. 3:14). But Jesus persisted, "Let it be so now; for it is proper for us in this way to fulfill all righteousness" (Matt. 3:15). Was this exchange simply placed in the mouths of John and Jesus to cover up the early Christians' embarrassment, or does it reveal something decisive about Jesus' identity and mission? In point of fact, the phrase "fulfill all

---

4. C.S. Lewis, *Mere Christianity* (New York: HarperCollins, 2001), 47.

righteousness" is a sort of scriptural code, designating both covenant and sacrifice. When Israel followed the covenantal requirements of the Lord, it became "righteous"—that is to say, correctly ordered—and when the repentant sinner performed a sacrifice, he recovered a lost righteousness. Jesus' words to the Baptist, therefore, signify that he has come to realize the covenant (union between divinity and humanity) precisely through a sacrificial participation in the condition of the sinner. In the manner of Isaiah's suffering servant, Jesus at the Jordan was identifying himself totally with the condition of sinners, announcing his intention to bear their burden and assume their guilt. He was, accordingly, the incarnation of God's own (rather embarrassing) humility and condescension. Just after the description of Jesus' baptism, we find in Matthew's Gospel an account of his confrontation with the tempter. Here we see what the identification with sinners, adumbrated at the baptism, looks like in practice. After forty days of fasting in the desert (evocative of Israel's forty years of wandering in the desert), Jesus meets the devil, who proceeds to lure the Messiah onto the path of sin. His sacrifice will entail his coming to battle sin at close quarters, his willingness, therefore, to be drawn by its power, to come under its sway. Satan first tempts him with sensual pleasure: "If you are the Son of God, command these stones to become loaves of bread" (Matt. 4:3). One of the most elemental forms of spiritual dysfunction is to make the satisfaction of sensual desire the center of one's life. Thus Jesus enters, through psychological and spiritual identification, into the condition of the person lured by this sin, but then he manages to withstand the temptation and in fact to twist this perversion back to rectitude: "One does not live by bread alone, but by every word that comes from the mouth of God" (Matt. 4:4). He does the same thing with the temptations to glory ("Do not put the Lord your God to the test" [Matt. 4:7]) and to power ("Worship the Lord your God, and serve only him" [Matt. 4:10]). If these perversions had been addressed only from a distance, only through divine fiat, they would not have been truly conquered; but when they are withstood by someone willing fully to submit to their lure, they are effectively exploded from within, undermined, defeated. This is the strategy of Jesus, the Lamb of God.

We see it in a number of Gospel scenes where Jesus is tired out after his contact with the sick, the lost, the sinful. At the beginning of Mark's Gospel, we find an account of a typical day in the ministry of Jesus. The people press on him from all sides, compelling him to find refuge in a boat lest he be crushed by the crowd, and at one point there are so many supplicants surrounding him that he couldn't even eat. Mark tells us that Jesus went off to a secluded place to pray, but even there they sought him out, coming at him from all sides. In the magnificent narrative of the woman at the well in the Gospel of John, we hear that Jesus sat down by Jacob's well, "tired out by his journey" (John 4:6). This description is straightforward enough on the literal level: Who wouldn't be tired after a morning's march through dry country? But as Augustine and others have reminded us, it has another sense on the mystical level. Jesus is tired from his incarnational journey into human sin and dysfunction, signified by the well. "You come to this well every day and you become thirsty again," Jesus says to the woman, indicating that the well is emblematic of errant desire, her tendency to fill up her longing for God with the transient goods of creation: money, pleasure, power, honor. In order to effect a change in her, the Lamb of God had to be willing to enter into her dysfunctional world and to share the spiritual weariness of it. J.R.R. Tolkien keenly appreciated the sacrificial dynamic that we've been exploring. His great Christ-figure, Frodo the hobbit, brought about the salvation of Middle-earth precisely through his entry into the heart of the land of Mordor, disempowering that terrible place through his humble willingness to bear the full weight of its burden.

All of this was, however, but an anticipation of the ultimate sacrifice of the Lamb of God. The final enemy that had to be defeated, if God and his human family could once again sit down in the easy fellowship of a festive meal, was death itself. In a very real sense, death (and the fear of death) stand behind all sin, and hence Jesus had to journey into the realm of death and, through sacrifice, twist it back to life. Innumerable heroes in the course of human history had tried to conquer that realm by using its weapons, fighting violence with violence and hatred with hatred. But this strategy was (and still is) hopeless. The battle plan of the Lamb of God was paradoxical in the extreme: he would conquer death precisely by dying. From Jesus' first appearance, the world (biblical shorthand for the arena of death) opposed him. Herod sought to stamp him out, even when he was an infant; the scribes and Pharisees plotted against him and hunted him down; the temple establishment feared him; the Romans saw him as a threat to right order. At the climax of his life and ministry, Jesus came into Jerusalem, David's city, the site of the temple, riding not on a fine charger in the manner of a worldly warrior, but on a humble donkey. He arrived in the place where his enemies were most concentrated, and he had every intention of fighting, but his weapon would be the very instrument on which his opponents would put him to death.

On the cross, Jesus said, "Father, forgive them, for they do not know what they are doing" (Luke 23:34). Dying on a Roman instrument of torture, he allowed the full force of the world's hatred and dysfunction to wash over him, to spend itself on him. And he responded, not with an answering violence or resentment, but with forgiveness. He therefore took away the sin of the world (to use the language of the liturgy), swallowing it up in the divine mercy. Over his cross, Pontius Pilate had placed a sign, announcing in Hebrew, Latin, and Greek that Jesus was the King of the Jews. Though Pilate meant it as mockery, it was in fact the fulfillment of a prophecy. An essential aspect of the hope of Israel was that one day a king in the tradition of David and Solomon would rise up, take his place in Jerusalem, and deal definitively with the enemies of the nation. This is precisely who Jesus was and precisely what Jesus did. But what an odd, unexpected sort of king he was, conquering Israel's enemies through nonviolence, disempowering them by refusing to respond to them in kind. In the Gospel of Luke, Jesus compared himself to a mother hen who longed to gather her chicks under her wing. As N.T. Wright points out, this is much more than a sentimental image. It refers to the gesture of a hen when fire is sweeping through the barn. In order to protect her chicks, she will sacrifice herself, gathering them under her wing and using her own body as a shield. On the cross, Jesus used, as it were, his own sacrificed body as a shield, taking the full force of the world's hatred and violence. He entered into close quarters with sin (because that's where we sinners are found) and allowed the heat and fury of sin to destroy him, even as he protected us. With this metaphor in mind, we can see, with special clarity, why the first Christians associated the crucified Jesus with the suffering servant of Isaiah. By enduring the pain of the cross, Jesus did indeed bear our sins; by his stripes we were indeed healed. And this is why the sacrificial death of Jesus is pleasing to the Father. Though it has in recent years been lampooned as advocating a type of divine child abuse, the doctrine of the atonement stands at the heart of Christian faith and proclamation. The Father sent his Son into godforsakenness, into the morass of sin and death, not because he delighted in seeing his Son suffer, but rather because he wanted his Son to bring the divine light to the darkest place. It is not the agony of the Son in itself that pleases his Father, but rather the Son's willing obedience in offering his body in sacrifice in order to take away the sin of the world. St. Anselm (the one most often blamed for propagating the theory of atonement) said that the death of the Son reestablished justice—that is to say, the right relationship between divinity and humanity.[5] He did it, Anselm continues, by going all the

---

5. *Cur Deus Homo* 1.9–11, in *Anselm: Basic Writings*, ed. and trans. Thomas Williams (Indianapolis, IN: Hackett, 2007), 255–262.

way to the bottom of the muck of sin in order to find and extricate the pearl (humanity) which had fallen in.[6] It was not the suffering of the Son per se that the Father loved, but rather the Son's willingness to make that downward journey.

The Eucharist as Sacrifice

It is only now, at the conclusion of this survey of practically the whole of salvation history, that we are in a position to understand the relationship between the Eucharist and sacrifice. This association is far from arbitrary or accidental, for it was made by Jesus himself, as he was summing up the meaning of his life in the company of his disciples on the night before his death. Luke tells us that, at his last great festive meal, Jesus "took a loaf of bread, and when he had given thanks, he broke it and gave it to them, saying, 'This is my body, which is given for you. Do this in remembrance of me'" (Luke 22:19). And then, at the conclusion of the meal, he took a cup of wine and said, "This cup that is poured out for you is the new covenant in my blood" (Luke 22:20). On Matthew's telling, Jesus makes the sacrificial significance even clearer: over the cup he says, "Drink from it, all of you; for this is my blood of the covenant, which is poured out for many for the forgiveness of sins" (Matt. 26:27–28).

In order to appreciate these perhaps overly familiar words, we have to put ourselves in the thought world of Jesus' first audience. As they heard these extraordinary statements, the Apostles were undoubtedly hearing overtones and resonances from the scriptural and liturgical tradition that we have reviewed. Jesus was using the Passover supper to give a definitive interpretation to the actions that he would take the next day, Good Friday. As this bread is broken and shared, so, he was saying, my body tomorrow will be broken and offered; as this cup is

---

6. Anselm, 1.19, 277.

poured out, so my blood tomorrow will be poured out in sacrifice. His body, he was implying, will be like the animals offered by Abraham when God struck a covenant with him, and his blood will be like the oxen's blood sprinkled by Moses on the altar and on the people, sealing the agreement of the Torah. In his crucified body, he will be like the Passover lamb slaughtered in the temple, signifying Israel's total commitment to Yahweh and Yahweh's to Israel. Moreover, his body will be like that of Isaac as he waited for the knife of his father to fall, with the telling difference that Jesus' Father will carry through the sacrifice. And if we attend carefully to the words over the cup, we can't help but see that his act on the cross will be the condition for the possibility of the perfect covenant of which Jeremiah dreamed. When Jesus said, "This cup is the new covenant in my blood," his disciples certainly thought of the promise that one day Yahweh would effect a fully realized union with his people. And when they heard that this covenant was to be accompanied by the shedding of blood, how could they not think of the link between Jeremiah's dream and the suffering servant of Isaiah? In sum, the words of Jesus over the bread and cup at the Last Supper effected a stunning gathering of the variety of strands of covenantal and sacrificial theology in the Hebrew Scriptures. The covenants and their accompanying sacrifices that mark the entire religious history of the Jews are being recapitulated, Jesus says, in me and my sacrifice. He undoubtedly knew that the horror of the Crucifixion would be so stark as to block any attempt to assign meaning to it. And thus, in the relative safety and intimacy of the upper room, Jesus calmly and in advance provided the interpretive key to the climactic action of his life. Why did Jesus invite his disciples to consume the bread and wine that he had radically identified with his sacrifice? In Jeremiah's prophecy of the new covenant, Yahweh had said, "I will put my law within them, and I will write it on their hearts" (Jer. 31:33). This means that the everlasting agreement would be written not on stone tablets but in the flesh of the people's hearts; it would not be an oppressive law externally imposed but a rule congruent with the deepest longing of the human soul. Jesus thus wanted them to ingest his sacrifice so as to appropriate it in the most intimate, organic way, making it bone of their bone and flesh of their flesh. Thomas Aquinas commented that the old Law of the Torah and the various covenants had a mitigated effectiveness, precisely because it appeared as external to the human heart. But, he continued, the new law of the Gospel is efficacious because it is realized internally, through the identification of Christ and his Body the Church.[7] And nowhere is this identification more complete than in the Eucharist, when a disciple physically consumes the incarnate Christ, the law par excellence.

We are now in a position to address more fully the issue that we raised at the outset of this chapter—namely, how the Mass can be construed as a sacrifice. We have already shown how the sacrifice of Jesus' cross sums up and gathers the sacrificial history that preceded it. The Mass, the Eucharistic liturgy, can be understood as an extension or re-presentation of the sacrifice of Jesus, bringing the power of the cross to bear in the present. Hence the Mass, in a very real sense, recapitulates and makes concrete everything we have been describing in the course of this chapter. If Jesus were one religious figure among many, an inspiring example from the past, we could gather now as his disciples and rather blandly remember him, much as the Abraham Lincoln Society might assemble and recall the virtues of the great president. Because of who Jesus is, however, something else obtains. The Mass is indeed described as an *anamnesis* (a remembrance) of the Last Supper and Calvary, but this term is meant in much more than a merely psychological sense. Since Jesus is divine, all of his actions, including and especially the sacrificial act by which he saved the world, participate in the eternity of God and hence can be made present at any point in time. To "remember" him, therefore, is to

---

7. Thomas Aquinas, *Summa theologiae* 1-2.107.1 ad 2 and 3.

participate even now in the saving events of the past, bringing them, in all of their dense reality to the present day. The Battle of Hastings cannot be re-presented, except in the most superficial sense, since it belongs irretrievably to the past, but the sacrifice of Jesus can. Those who are gathered around the altar of Christ are not simply recalling Calvary; Calvary has become present to them in all of its spiritual power. Due to the eternity of Christ, there is indeed a kind of collapsing of the dimensions of time at the Mass, present meeting past—and both present and past anticipating the eschatological future. St. Paul caught this trans-temporality of the Eucharistic liturgy beautifully when, in his First Letter to the Corinthians, he said, "As often as you eat this bread and drink the cup, you proclaim the Lord's death until he comes" (1 Cor. 11:26). In other words, here and now, at the Eucharistic assembly, Christ makes present both the past and the future. Indeed, the whole sacrificial history of Israel—from Noah and Abraham through David and Isaiah and Jesus himself—is gathered and summed up, re-presented at the Mass.

Martin Luther and the other reformers objected strenuously to the claim that the Mass was a sacrifice. Luther argued that Christ's great sacrifice was once for all and that if we, consequently, arrogate to ourselves the prerogative of repeating it, we are guilty of dangerous spiritual presumptuousness, or in his language, "righteousness of works." The Mass, he concluded, is something that is received, not offered, by us. What we have just said about the time-transcending quality of Jesus' act goes a long way toward dissolving Luther's criticism, for we are not repeating Christ's sacrifice on our own terms and through our own initiative; rather we are, as we've said, re-presenting it, tapping into its power. But we can take another step in responding to Luther's concern. The God of the Bible is not competitive with us. As we argued in the first chapter, God the Creator of all things cannot possibly receive anything from creation that he needs. But God does indeed desire something for his human creatures—namely, fullness of life—and this comes when they surrender themselves in love to him. The sacrifice of Jesus is nothing but this total self-gift to the Father that effectively straightens out the human race, and therefore God is delighted when we actively participate in it, joining our minds, wills, and bodies to it. The sacrifice of the Mass does not constitute a challenge to God; rather, it breaks, as it were, against the rock of God's self-sufficiency and returns to us as a life-enhancing power.

The most compelling biblical depiction of Jesus as sacrificial priest is found in the Letter to the Hebrews. The author of this treatise interpreted Jesus in the context of the ritual and ceremonial of the Jerusalem temple, of which he himself was probably a priest. As we saw, the high priest went every year into the Holy of Holies to make atonement for the sins of the people and to bring forth the divine forgiveness. As such, he was a "pontifex," a bridge builder between divinity and humanity. Nowhere in the New Testament is the coming together of the divine and human in Jesus more clearly articulated than in this letter. We are told that Jesus is "the reflection of God's glory and the exact imprint of God's very being, and he sustains all things by his powerful word" (Heb. 1:3). At the same time, we are assured, "he had to become like his brothers and sisters in every respect. . . . Because he himself was tested by what he suffered, he is able to help those who are being tested" (Heb. 2:17–18). This juxtaposition of divinity and humanity made Jesus the unsurpassably perfect high priest, able "to make a sacrifice of atonement for the sins of the people" (Heb. 2:17). But whereas the ordinary high priests of the Old Testament passed through the veil into the earthly Holy of Holies and offered, at best, an inadequate sacrifice, the perfect high priest passed into the heavenly sanctuary, bearing the sins of the world and bringing forth, in the fullest sense, the divine forgiveness: "But when Christ came as a high priest of the good things that have come . . . he entered once for all into the Holy Place, not with the blood of goats and calves, but with his own blood, thus obtaining eternal redemption" (Heb. 9:11–12). The author of the Letter to the Hebrews, so immersed in the Old Testament texts, makes the explicit connection between sacrifice and covenant that I have been insisting on throughout this chapter: "For this reason [Christ] is the mediator of a new covenant, so that those who are called may receive the promised eternal inheritance" (Heb. 9:15). We recall that God had promised Abraham countless descendants and David an everlasting line of kings. Now in Christ we see the unexpected fulfillment of these covenant promises. Through the final sacrifice of Jesus the high priest, eternal life has been made available to the whole of humanity and the covenant thereby realized beyond the wildest fantasies of Abraham, Moses, Isaiah, or David.

The sacrifice of the Mass is a participation in this great eternal act by which Jesus entered on our behalf into the heavenly sanctuary with his own blood and returned bearing the forgiveness of the Father. When the high priest came out of the sanctuary and sprinkled the people with blood, he was understood to be acting in the very person of Yahweh, renewing creation. The ultimate sacrifice having been offered, Christ the priest comes forth at every Mass with his lifeblood, and the universe is restored. The priest's actions at the altar are but a symbolic manifestation of this mystical reality, which is why he is described as operating *in persona Christi* (in the person of Christ). And this is why, furthermore, the forgiveness of sins is so central to the Eucharistic liturgy. Though it isn't stressed enough, all of our venial sins (that is to say, those sins that have not involved a radical compromising of our relationship with God and hence rendered us spiritually dead) are washed away by Christ's Blood at Mass. As the guests at Babette's feast felt their animosities and resentments die away due to the sacrifice of Babette, so we experience the forgiveness of our sins when Christ's sacrificial Blood is offered to us.

The Vatican II document on the Church, *Lumen Gentium*, says that every baptized person is a priest—that is to say, someone capable of entering into the sacrificial dynamic of the liturgy. Though the ordained priest alone can preside at the Mass and effect the Eucharistic change, all of the baptized participate in the Mass in a priestly way. They do this through their prayers and responses but also, the document specifies, by uniting their personal sacrifices and sufferings to the great sacrifice of Christ.[8] So a father witnesses the agony of his son in the hospital; a mother endures the rebellion of a teenage daughter; a young man receives news of his brother's death in battle; an elderly man tosses on his bed in anxiety as he contemplates his unsure financial situation; a graduate student struggles to complete his doctoral thesis; a child experiences for the first time the breakup of a close friendship; an idealist confronts the stubborn resistance of a cynical opponent. These people could see their pain as simply dumb suffering, the offscourings of an indifferent universe. Or they could see it through the lens provided by the sacrificial death of Jesus, appreciating it as the means by which God is drawing them closer to himself. Suffering, once joined to the cross of Jesus, can become a vehicle for the reformation of the sinful self, the turning of the soul in the direction of love. Mind you, I am not suggesting a simplistic causal correlation between sin and suffering (indeed, the book of Job rules out such a move); but I *am* suggesting that pain, consciously aligned to the sacrifice of Jesus, can be spiritually transfiguring. Thus, the sufferer becomes, not simply a person in pain, but Abraham giving away what he loves the most, Moses enduring the long discipline of the desert, David confronting Goliath and being pursued by Saul, or the crucified Messiah wondering why he has been forsaken by the Father. The place where this alignment happens is the liturgy, for the liturgy is the re-presentation of the sacrifice of the Lord in all of its richness and multivalence. Consequently, those who gather, with intentionality and focus, at the altar of Jesus are not simply witnessing

---

8. See *Lumen Gentium*, nos. 10–11, in *The Word on Fire Vatican II Collection* (Park Ridge, IL: Word on Fire Institute, 2021), 57–59.

the event of the cross; they are sharing in it. And this participation changes fundamentally the manner in which they experience and interpret their own pain.

And thus we can see, finally and fully, the intimate link between the meal and the sacrifice aspects of the Eucharist. Only in the measure that we are transformed through sacrifice, only when our sin and suffering have been dealt with, can we sit down in the fellowship of the sacred banquet. And thus we have come full circle. The Eucharistic liturgy is the sacred meal *because* it is a sacrificial offering. In the Blood of Jesus, the bliss of Eden is restored, and God and human beings are once again friends.

Chapter 3

"IF IT'S A SYMBOL,
TO HELL WITH IT"

In 1950, Flannery O'Connor was brought by friends to a dinner with the prominent author Mary McCarthy and her husband. At the time, O'Connor, who would eventually blossom into one of the greatest Catholic writers of the twentieth century, was just commencing her career, and there was no question but that she was a junior member of this elite circle of conversation. In fact, in a letter describing the scene, she commented, "Having me there was like having a dog present who had been trained to say a few words but overcome with inadequacy had forgotten them." As the evening drew on, the talk turned to the Eucharist, and Mary McCarthy, who had been raised Catholic but had fallen away from the Church, remarked that she thought of the Eucharist as a symbol and "implied that it was a pretty good one." She undoubtedly intended this condescending observation as a friendly overture to the Catholic O'Connor. But O'Connor responded in a shaky voice, "Well, if it's a symbol, to hell with it."[1] One can only imagine that the elegant dinner party broke up rather soon after that conversational bomb was dropped. In its bluntness, clarity, and directness, Flannery O'Connor's remark is one

---

1. Flannery O'Connor, *The Habit of Being: Letters of Flannery O'Connor* (New York: Farrar, Straus & Giroux, 1979), 125. Quoted in *Flannery O'Connor Collection* (Park Ridge, IL: Word on Fire Classics, 2019), 157.

of the best statements of the Catholic difference in regard to the Eucharist. For Catholics, the Eucharist *is* the Body and Blood of Jesus, and any attempt to say otherwise, no matter how cleverly formulated or deftly articulated, is insufficient.

O'Connor's *bon mot* reflects what the Catholic Church speaks of in its doctrinal statements as the "Real Presence" of Christ in the Eucharist. As the Vatican II fathers pointed out, Christ is indeed present in a variety of ways—in the very intelligibility of the universe, in the gathered assembly at Mass, in the reading of the Scriptures, in the person of the priest—but he is "really, truly, and substantially" present, that is to say, present in a qualitatively different way, in the Eucharistic elements. In the Middle Ages, Thomas Aquinas gave voice to the same conviction when he said that whereas the power (*virtus*) of Christ is operative in the other sacraments, Christ himself (*ipse Christus*) is present in the sacrament of the altar.[2] We recall that, in "Babette's Feast," one of the sisters made the connection between the missionary who had dined, unknowingly, on the native chief's grandson and the guests at her staid Lutheran table who had dined, without realizing it, on the very substance of Babette. The *reality* of Babette's self-offering in love, she concluded, had made the communion of that banquet table possible. O'Connor, Aquinas, the fathers of Vatican II, and Dinesen are all indicating that the intertwining of meal and sacrifice at the Eucharist is made possible by the dense objectivity of what is on offer there. If Christ's presence in the Eucharist is only symbolic, then the sacrifice is mitigated, and if the sacrifice is mitigated, the communion is compromised. In a word, the Real Presence is the glue that holds together the elements that we've been considering. But what precisely does this "Real Presence" mean, and what is the ground for holding it? Once again, I would like to answer these questions from within a biblical framework.

---

2. Thomas Aquinas, *Summa theologiae* 3.62.5, 3.73.5.

The Scandal of John 6

I mentioned earlier that all four Gospels have an account of the multiplication of the loaves and fishes. St. John's version of this story can be found at the beginning of the sixth chapter of his Gospel. In his telling, immediately after performing this miracle, Jesus fled to a mountain and then crossed the Sea of Galilee, pursued by a crowd eager to see more wonders and to make the wonder-worker into a king. They finally tracked him down in the synagogue in the lakeside town of Capernaum, and there a remarkable dialogue ensued. In many ways, the Catholic doctrine of the Real Presence flows from and continually returns to this conversation. Thus, we must attend to it with particular care.

When they asked Jesus how he had gotten there ahead of them, the Lord chided them: "Very truly, I tell you, you are looking for me, not because you saw signs, but because you ate your fill of the loaves. Do not work for the food that perishes, but for the food that endures for eternal life" (John 6:26–27). Ordinary bread satisfies only physical longing, and it does so in a transient way: one eats and one must soon eat again. But the heavenly bread, Jesus implies, satisfies the deepest longing of the heart, and does so by adapting the one who eats it to eternal life. The Church Fathers loved to ruminate on this theme of divinization through the Eucharist, the process by which the consumption of the bread of life readies one for life in the eternal dimension. In the versions of the Lord's prayer found in the synoptic Gospels, we find the phrase *ton arton . . . ton epiousion,* usually rendered as "daily bread." But the literal sense of the Greek is something like "supersubstantial bread," designating, not so much the bread of ordinary human consumption, but the bread suitable for a higher pitch of existence.

As is often the case in the Gospel of John, a skeptical question opens toward deeper understanding: "So they said to him, 'What sign are you going to give us then, so that we may see it and believe you? . . . Our ancestors ate the manna in the wilderness'" (John 6:30–31).

They were appealing, of course, to the miracle by which Yahweh fed the children of Israel during their forty years' wandering in the desert, but Jesus wants them to understand that he is offering a food that will nourish them in a more abiding way. "Your ancestors ate the manna in the wilderness, and they died. This is the bread that comes down from heaven, so that one may eat of it and not die" (John 6:49–50). "Heavenly bread" catches much of the paradox of the orthodox teaching concerning the Eucharist: though it remains, as far as the eye can see, ordinary bread, the Eucharist in fact participates in a properly transcendent mode of existence and possesses, consequently, the power to produce eternal life. In Jesus' next observation, we see precisely why the heavenly bread has this virtue: "I am the living bread that came down from heaven. Whoever eats of this bread will live forever; and the bread that I will give for the life of the world is my flesh" (John 6:51). Here again we see that stubborn realism upon which the Catholic tradition will insist. Jesus unambiguously identifies himself with this bread that will nourish his people to eternal life.

What follows is one of the most beautifully understated lines in the Gospel of John: "The Jews disputed among themselves, saying, 'How can this man give us his flesh to eat?'" (John 6:52). I say "understated," for the term "dispute" barely hints at the intensity of the objections that must have come forward from the crowd upon hearing Jesus' words. They must have found this discourse, not only intellectually and religiously problematic, but if I can put it this bluntly, nauseating. Throughout the Old Testament, we can find numerous explicit prohibitions against the eating of flesh and blood. For example, in the book of Genesis, in the context of the Noah story, we find this divine directive: "Every moving thing that lives shall be food for you; and just as I gave you the green plants, I give you everything. Only, you shall not eat flesh with its life, that is, its blood" (Gen. 9:3–4). The idea here is that since blood is the vital principle that belongs to God alone, it ought not to be brought under the control of human beings.

We find the same prohibition among the legal decrees in the books of Leviticus and Deuteronomy: "It shall be a perpetual statute through your generations, in all of your settlements: you must not eat any fat or any blood" (Lev. 3:17), and "Only be sure that you do not eat the blood; for the blood is the life, and you shall not eat the life with the meat" (Deut. 12:23). Moreover, in his vision of apocalyptic judgment, the prophet Ezekiel speaks of the carrion birds who will swoop down on the enemies of Israel and eat their flesh and drink their blood: "You shall eat the flesh of the mighty, and drink the blood of the princes of the earth. . . . You shall eat fat until you are filled and drink blood until you are drunk" (Ezek. 39:18–19). Finally, a popular Aramaic saying of Jesus' time identified the devil as the "eater of flesh."[3] If the prohibitions we have rehearsed had to do with the consumption of the bloody flesh of animals, how much more offensive must Jesus' words have been, which encouraged the eating of his own human body. Hence the visceral negative reaction of Jesus' audience.

If Jesus, therefore, wanted to soften his teaching, to place it in a wider interpretive context, to insist upon the metaphorical or symbolic sense of the words he was using, this would have been the perfect opportunity. As I mentioned, the skeptical questions of his interlocutors are often the occasion, in John's Gospel, for Jesus to clarify the meaning of his pronouncements. A very good example is his symbolic explanation of the sense of "being born from above" when confronted with the literalistic question of Nicodemus, "Can one enter a second time into the mother's womb and be born?" (John 3:3–5). But in this case, Jesus didn't spiritualize his rhetoric; just the contrary. He said, "Very truly, I tell you, unless you eat the flesh of the Son of Man and drink his blood, you have no life in you" (John 6:53). Behind the English term "eat" in this sentence is not the Greek word we would expect, *phagein*, which means to eat in the ordinary sense. The term

---

3. See Raymond E. Brown, *The Gospel According to John I–XII* (New York: Doubleday, 1966), 284.

that is used is *trogein,* which was typically employed to communicate the manner in which animals consume their food; it might be rendered as "gnaw" or "munch" in English. Thus, if they were bothered by the gross animalistic overtones of what he had said, he purposely bothered them further. And in case they still missed his meaning, he added, "for my flesh is true food and my blood is true drink" (John 6:55).

He then draws the crucial conclusion from all of this bluntly realistic talk: "Those who eat my flesh and drink my blood abide in me, and I in them. Just as the living Father sent me, and I live because of the Father, so whoever eats me will live because of me" (John 6:56–57). For Christians, Jesus is not simply a wise teacher by whose words one abides (like Confucius) or an ethical exemplar whom one might strive to follow (like Gandhi or St. Francis) or even a bearer of definitive revelation to whom a person might feel beholden (like Muhammad); rather, Jesus is a power in whom we participate, a field of force in which we live and move and have our being. In his master metaphor, St. Paul speaks of the body of Jesus of which baptized people are members. The rhetoric that we have just cited implies an intensely organic relationship between the Father, Jesus, and the Church, the third deriving its life from the second who derives his life from the first. We must eat the Flesh and drink the Blood of the Lord because that is the way that we come to participate in him and thus, finally, in the life of the Father. Elsewhere in John's Gospel, we find equally vitalistic language: we are much more than followers of Jesus; we are grafted onto him as branches are grafted onto a vine. The very earliest theology of the Eucharist is found in Paul's First Letter to the Corinthians, penned probably in the early fifties of the first century, and it clearly brings forth this organic, participative quality. Paul speaks of the intense identification that is affected between Jesus and his Church precisely through the Eucharist: "The cup of blessing that we bless, is it not a sharing in the blood of Christ? The bread that we break, is it not a sharing in the body of Christ" (1 Cor. 10:16)?

The evocative Greek term behind "sharing" is *koinonia,* meaning communion or mystical participation.

Is this a hard doctrine? At the conclusion of the Eucharistic discourse, delivered at the synagogue in Capernaum, Jesus practically lost his entire Church: "When many of his disciples heard it, they said, 'This teaching is difficult; who can accept it?'" (John 6:60). Again, if he were speaking only at the symbolic level, why would this theology be hard to accept? No one left him when he observed that he was the vine or the good shepherd or the light of the world, for those were clearly only metaphorical remarks and posed, accordingly, no great intellectual challenge. The very resistance of his disciples to the bread of life discourse implies that they understood Jesus only too well and grasped that he was making a qualitatively different kind of assertion. Unable to take in the Eucharistic teaching, "many of his disciples turned back and no longer went about with him" (John 6:66). Jesus then turned to his inner circle, the Twelve, and asked, bluntly enough: "Do you also wish to go away?" (John 6:67). There is something terrible and telling in that question, as though Jesus were posing it not only to the little band gathered around him at Capernaum, but to all of his prospective disciples up and down the ages. One senses that we are poised here on a fulcrum, that a standing or falling point has been reached, that somehow being a disciple of Jesus is intimately tied up with how one stands in regard to the Eucharist. In response to Jesus' question, Peter, as is often the case in the Gospels, spoke for the group: "Lord, to whom can we go? You have the words of eternal life. We have come to believe and know that you are the Holy One of God" (John 6:68–69). As in the synoptic Gospels, so here in John, it is a Petrine confession that grounds and guarantees the survival of the Church. In the Johannine context, this explicit confession of Jesus as the Holy One of God is bound up with the implicit confession of faith in the Eucharist as truly the Body and Blood of the Lord. When the two declarations are made in tandem, John is telling us, the Church perdures. In light of this scene, it is indeed fascinating to remark how often the Church has divided precisely over this question of the Real Presence.

The Witness of the Church Fathers
and the Argument with Berengarius

The great theologians of the early centuries of the Church's life wrote frequently about the Eucharist, but not in a systematic way. We find no treatises devoted precisely to the Eucharistic mystery until the early Middle Ages. But if we attend to the numerous citations, sprinkled here and there in the writings of the Fathers, we remark a number of central themes, including covenant, meal, and sacrifice. And we will also find—though again, not articulated in a nuanced way—affirmations of the Real Presence. Echoing a central motif of the sixth chapter of John, Ignatius of Antioch, writing to fellow Christians around the year 107 while he was journeying toward his own execution, spoke of the Eucharist as the bread that confers eternal life: "medicine of immortality."[4] If Ignatius thought that the Eucharist were ordinary bread, carrying only a symbolic valence, he would scarcely have imagined that it possessed such transformative power. In his *Epistle to the Romans,* furthermore, Ignatius says, "I desire the bread of God, the heavenly bread, the bread of life, which is the flesh of Jesus Christ, the Son of God, who became afterwards of the seed of David and Abraham; and I desire the drink of God, namely his blood, which is incorruptible love and eternal life."[5] Again, it's hard to imagine that such passionate language could be used of something that Ignatius considered merely a conventional sign. Around the year 150, Justin Martyr wrote a moving account of what Christians do at their Sunday worship. In the context of that description, he said this of the Eucharist: "This food is called among us Εὐχαριστία [the

4. Ignatius of Antioch, *Epistle to the Ephesians* 20 (*ANF* 1:58).
5. Ignatius of Antioch, *Epistle to the Romans* 7 (*ANF* 1:77).

Eucharist], of which no one is allowed to partake but the man who believes that the things which we teach are true. . . . The food which is blessed by the prayer of his word . . . is the flesh and blood of that Jesus who was made flesh."[6] Justin also repeats Ignatius' insistence that the Eucharist, precisely as the Body and Blood of the Lord, immortalizes the one who receives it.

Another early witness to the Real Presence is St. Irenaeus, a student of Polycarp of Smyrna, who later became bishop of Lyons and who died, probably as a martyr, in 202. Irenaeus' principal intellectual opponents were the Gnostics of whom I spoke in the opening chapter. One of the marks of their dualist system was, we recall, a contempt for matter. Accordingly, Irenaeus placed a great stress on the corporeal reality of the Incarnation and, by extension, of the Eucharist. In the fourth book of his masterpiece *Against Heresies,* Irenaeus magnificently combines the two beliefs and manages to refute the Gnostics in one deftly crafted rhetorical question: "How can they say that the bread over which thanks has been given is the Lord's Body and the cup His Blood, when they will not admit that that same Lord is the Son of the world's Creator, that is, His Word, through whom trees bear fruit . . . and 'the earth gives first the blade, then the ear, then the full grain in the ear' (Mark 4:28)?"[7] For our purposes, what is remarkable here is the clear and unambiguous affirmation that the dense reality of the Body and Blood of Christ in the Eucharist is a sacramental prolongation of the equally dense physical reality of the Incarnation.

Origen of Alexandria was a younger contemporary of Irenaeus and the greatest biblical theologian of his time. Based in Alexandria and Palestine, he produced a staggering number of commentaries, treatises, and sermons, all centering around the Word of God. Trying to

---

6. Justin Martyr, *The First Apology* 66 (*ANF* 1:185).
7. Irenaeus, *Against Heresies* 4.18.4, quoted in Hans Urs von Balthasar, *The Scandal of the Incarnation: Irenaeus Against the Heresies,* trans. John Saward (San Francisco: Ignatius Press, 1990), 92.

communicate something of his enormous reverence for the Scriptures, Origen used a comparison that, in regard to the question under consideration, is extremely illuminating. He told his listeners: "You who are accustomed to take part in divine mysteries know, when you receive the body of the Lord, how you protect it with all caution and veneration lest any small part fall from it, lest anything of the consecrated gift be lost."[8] In the same way, he urged them, you must strive to conserve and reverence every word of the revealed text. If Origen and his community held the Eucharistic bread to be nothing but a symbol, why would they even think of treating it with such exaggerated respect? And the very fact that this practice could be employed so blithely as a point of comparison proves that belief in the Real Presence was, even at this early period, utterly taken for granted.

One of the most precious texts that we have from the patristic period is a series of catechetical talks prepared by Cyril of Jerusalem. In these theologically rich sermons, Cyril was attempting to draw newly baptized Christians into the central mysteries of the faith. When discussing the Eucharist, he directs his listeners' attention to a text from First Corinthians: "For I received from the Lord what I also handed on to you, that the Lord Jesus on the night when he was betrayed took a loaf of bread, and when he had given thanks, he broke it and said, 'This is my body that is for you.' . . . In the same way he took the cup also, after supper, saying, 'This cup is the new covenant in my blood'" (1 Cor. 11:23–25). Cyril comments, emphasizing the organic nature of Eucharistic participation: "The teaching of the Blessed Paul is sufficient to give you a full assurance concerning those Divine Mysteries, of which having been deemed worthy, you have become of the same body and blood with Christ." And lest there be any ambiguity, he adds, "Since [Christ] has himself

---

8. Origen of Alexandria, *Homilies on Genesis and Exodus*, ed. Hermigild Dressler, trans. Ronald E. Heine (Washington, DC: The Catholic University of America Press, 1982), 380–381.

affirmed and said, This is my Blood, who shall ever hesitate, saying, that it is not his Blood?"[9]

In the fourth century, St. Ambrose of Milan added his voice to the chorus. To those who wondered about the reality of Christ's bodily presence in the Eucharist, he said, "This body which we make is that which was born of the Virgin," and to those who inquired as to the truth of the Eucharistic transformation, he said, "Before the blessing of the heavenly words another nature [bread] is spoken of; after the consecration the Body is signified."[10] St. John Chrysostom, the eloquent fourth-century bishop of Constantinople, bore as one of his titles "Eucharistic Doctor," since he wrote so frequently and passionately about the mystery of Christ's Body and Blood. In one of his homilies, he remarks on the power necessary to effect the Eucharistic transformation: "It is not man that causes the things offered to become the Body and Blood of Christ, but he who was crucified for us. . . . The priest, in the role of Christ, pronounces these words, but their power and grace are God's."[11] If Chrysostom and Ambrose considered the Eucharist merely a symbolic representation of Jesus' Body and Blood, they would never have insisted on the necessity of divine power in the words of consecration. There is no reason whatsoever that an ordinary human being could not bring about a new symbolic state of affairs: writers, poets, and artists do it all the time. Thus, their allusions to the power of God's grace in and through the words of consecration is an indirect indication that they believed something much more than merely symbolic was at play in the Eucharist.

And the greatest of the Western Fathers, St. Augustine of Hippo, also held to the dense objectivity of Christ's Eucharistic presence. In the

9. Cyril of Jerusalem, *Catechetical Lectures* 22.1 (*NPNF²* 7:151).
10. Ambrose of Milan, *On the Mysteries* 9.53–54 (*NPNF²* 10:324).
11. John Chrysostom, *In proditionem Judae* (On the betrayal of Judas) 1.6 (PG 49:380), translation from the *Catechism of the Catholic Church*, 1375.

line of Origen, Ambrose, Chrysostom, and others, Augustine maintains that the consecratory words of Jesus have a transformative power, so that when they are pronounced over the bread and wine at Mass, a very real change takes place. In one of his homilies, he comments, "That which you see on the Lord's table is bread and wine. But when a word is added, that bread and wine become the body and blood of the Word. . . . Without the word, the oblation is bread and wine, but, when the word is added, the oblation is at once something else. And that something else—what is it? It is the body of Christ and the blood of Christ."[12] Once more, this sort of rhetoric is incompatible with the view that the Eucharistic change is merely figurative, for no one thinks that the ontological constitution of an object mutates when a symbolic meaning is attached to it. But this is precisely what Augustine and his forebears did indeed hold.

This patristic consensus on the Real Presence emerged in the course of several centuries, but never during this period did any of the masters of Christian thought endeavor to explain the "how" of the Eucharistic change, beyond their insistence that the word of Christ was its necessary condition. But during the Carolingian period, when Christianity's intellectual center of gravity shifted to the north and the west, theologians began to pose more technical questions about the Eucharist and attempted to state in more philosophically adequate language what happens when Christ becomes really present in the elements at Mass. Some scholars, in recent years, have bemoaned this development, seeing it as a descent into a fussy physicalism and have called, consequently, for a return to the more poetic and lyrical approach of the Bible and the Fathers. But this, I think, is a mistake, for the intellectual move from the "what" and the "why" to the "how" is a natural one, and thus even if we wanted to undo it, we couldn't.

---

12. Augustine, *Commentary on the Lord's Sermon on the Mount with Seventeen Related Sermons*, ed. Hermigild Dressler, trans. Denis J. Kavanagh (Washington, DC: The Catholic University of America Press, 2010), 321, 325.

And in point of fact, the exploration of the more "technical" dimension of the Eucharist, when undertaken in the right spirit, preserves rather than undermines the mystery of the sacrament.

The most important Eucharistic debate of this period centered around the work of Berengarius of Tours, an eleventh-century theologian. Like many of the other intellectuals of the time, Berengarius was fascinated by grammar and the logical property of terms, and he posed a simple but penetrating logical objection to the belief in Jesus' Real Presence in the Eucharist. Berengarius claimed that there is an essential difference between the historical body of Jesus, born of the Virgin and now reigning in heaven, and the "body" that appears sacramentally on the altar. This latter must be, he reckoned, some sort of symbol or figure of the former, since the heavenly body of Jesus is beyond change or corruption, whereas the Eucharistic elements are, obviously enough, changed and corrupted over time. A scriptural *locus* for Berengarius is the Pauline claim that "even though we once knew Christ from a human point of view, we know him no longer in that way" (2 Cor. 5:16). In his own commentary on this passage, Berengarius said that the words of the Apostle were a refutation "of anyone who says: 'The empirical [*sensualis*] bread consecrated on the altar is, after the consecration, truly the body of Christ that exists above.'"[13] And therefore, when the priest at Mass says *hoc est enim corpus meum* (this indeed is my body), the *hoc* in question remains the bread, but a spiritual significance or power (*virtus*) is added to it, making it an efficacious sign of the body of Jesus. One can say that the bread and wine are truly the Body and Blood of Christ in the sense that the risen Christ is offered spiritually to the recipient through them.

Grammatically, Berengarius' argument is interesting. In any change, there must be a substrate—that is to say, something that

---

13. Berengarius of Tours, *De sacra coena adversus Lanfrancum* 27, ed. Willem Hermanus Beekenkamp (The Hague, 1941), 58. Translation from Jaroslav Pelikan, *The Christian Tradition: A History of the Development of Doctrine*, vol. 3, *The Growth of Medieval Theology (600–1300)* (Chicago: University of Chicago Press, 1978), 192.

remains stable throughout the transition: it is the same person, for example, who stays the same even as he puts on a variety of different shirts. What Berengarius points out is that if the Eucharistic elements cease to exist at the consecration, no real change is in fact possible. The *hoc* (this) in the priest's formula requires, therefore, the permanence of the bread and wine. When he says, furthermore, that a virtue or spiritual power is added to the elements, Berengarius anticipates by several centuries the work of Martin Luther. The great reformer will argue that the body of Christ comes to exist alongside of the bread and the blood of Christ alongside the wine, so that neither bread nor wine pass out of existence or become something essentially different at the consecration. Berengarius, like Luther after him, feels that he can account for the densely realistic claims of the Bible and the Fathers since, "whatever is said to be the case spiritually is truly the case."[14] One has to admit, I think, that there is something attractive in the clarity and simplicity of Berengarius' presentation of the Eucharist. It takes the Eucharistic change seriously without mystifying it; it sets this sacramental transition within the familiar context of symbolic change, aligning it with other instances from our ordinary experience. The doubt that nags at us whenever we consider the doctrine of the *Real* Presence is largely assuaged through Berengarius' intellectual ministrations.

Nevertheless, the theory of Berengarius met almost immediately with strenuous opposition. One of its most articulate critics was Lanfranc of Bec, a Benedictine abbot and a mentor to St. Anselm of Canterbury. Relying on John 6 and on the steady witness of the Fathers, Lanfranc maintained that Berengarius' approach was far too subjectivistic, far too cavalier about the *reality* of the Eucharistic change. When the controversy between Berengarius and Lanfranc began to disturb the Church at large, Pope Nicholas II called a synod

---

14. Berengarius of Tours, *Apologia*, in *Un testo inedito di Berengario di Tours e il Concilio Romano del 1079*, ed. Martinio Matronola (Milan, 1936), 120. Translation from Pelikan, *The Christian Tradition*, 186.

in 1059. At the end of the deliberations, the theology of Berengarius was condemned, and he himself was compelled to sign a recantation and acquiesce in the burning of his books. As part of his recantation, he was forced to admit that "the bread and wine which are placed on the altar are after consecration not only a sacrament but also the true body and blood of our Lord Jesus Christ."[15] This, as we've been suggesting, was the neuralgic point. The synod fathers recognized that at the consecration a change so dramatic and thorough occurs that it would be incorrect to refer to the elements afterward as "bread and wine." Berengarius' symbolic explanation did not account sufficiently for this radically objective transformation. They also insisted that there is something "more" in the Eucharist than in the other sacraments. One could argue, they implied, that Berengarius presented a valid account of the presence of Jesus in the sacraments of Baptism, Confirmation, the Anointing of the Sick, etc., wherein a spiritual power is added to a physical element. The oath that Berengarius was forced to take reflected the Church's instinct that something qualitatively different is at play in the Eucharist, a presence at a substantially different level of intensity. Moreover, Berengarius' theory couldn't account for the essential difference between the Eucharist and the wide range of symbolic signs in the Old Testament revelation, from the temple to cultic sacrifice to priestly ritual.

Now, there was more in the oath that Berengarius was forced to swear, and it makes even the opponents of Berengarius to this day rather uneasy: "The bread and wine . . . [are] the true body and blood of our Lord Jesus Christ and . . . are taken and broken by the hands of the priests and crushed by the teeth of the faithful."[16] The frank, even gross, physicality of this formula seems an over-corrective to the too subjectivistic theory of Berengarius, drawing us close to an almost

---

15. Quoted in Paul Bradshaw and Maxwell Johnson, *The Eucharistic Liturgies: Their Evolution and Interpretation* (Collegeville, MN: Liturgical Press, 2012), 224.

16. Bradshaw and Johnson, 225.

cannibalistic construal of the Eucharistic meal. In fact, in later polemics, the extreme view represented by the anti-Berengarian oath will be characterized as "Capernaitic," because the people in the Capernaum synagogue described in John 6 reacted against the grossly physical idea of "eating" the flesh of Jesus. The tension between Berengarius' excessively subjectivist reading and his opponents' excessively objectivistic interpretation establishes the poles between which the later tradition will attempt to negotiate in its articulation of the Eucharistic mystery.

Now, what precisely did Berengarius' opponents propose as an alternative explanation of the Real Presence? When we consult the works of Lanfranc, we find the first major attempt to explain Christ's presence in the Eucharistic elements through the concepts of "substance" and "accident" found in the philosophy of Aristotle. In his *Categories,* copies of which were present in several key monastic libraries of the eleventh century, Aristotle argued that the most basic metaphysical reality is primary substance, an intelligible substrate that lies "underneath" the various accidents of color, shape, size, position, and so forth that qualify it. Thus, a horse (substance) is large, brown, running, in front of another horse, etc. (its accidents). Aristotle's pithy definition of the two terms is as follows: a substance is that which is *neither* present in nor predicable of another, whereas an accident is that which is *either* present in or predicable of another. Armed with this Aristotelian perspective, Lanfranc could make some sense of the Eucharistic change. While the secondary qualities of the bread and wine—color, shape, size, aroma—remain unchanged, their underlying, and essentially invisible, substances are transformed into the Body and Blood of Christ. This conceptual innovation allowed the opponents of Berengarius to move beyond a purely figurative interpretation without embracing a crude physicalistic reading.

This eleventh-century debate eventually influenced the official teaching of the Catholic Church. In 1202, Pope Innocent III—certainly the most consequential pontiff of the Middle Ages—used the term "transubstantiation" for the first time in an official ecclesial document, when discussing the use of water and wine at the Eucharist. He remarked that some hold the water to be *transsubstantiatur in sanguinem* (transubstantiated into blood) in the process of consecration.[17] What is intriguing is how casually the pope used the word, indicating that it was already common parlance. Then, at the Fourth Lateran Council, which took place just thirteen years later, the term is employed, but again in an almost casual, taken-for-granted manner: The "Body and Blood [of Jesus Christ] are truly contained in the sacrament of the altar under the appearances of bread and wine, the bread being transubstantiated into the body by the divine power and the wine into the blood."[18] Undefined and relegated to a position within a subordinate clause, the term is obviously, by this time, generally accepted as an ordinary way of speaking about the Eucharistic change. But there is something more here as well. This very vagueness and lack of definition will be characteristic of official ecclesial usages of the term from this point on, since the Church never wanted to identify itself too strongly with a particular philosophical position or mode of explanation. Though it will consistently use a word marked by Aristotle's philosophy, the Church by no means ties itself thereby to Aristotelian metaphysics in the articulation of its Eucharistic faith.

The Eucharistic Theology of Thomas Aquinas

Called the "common doctor" of the Catholic Church, Thomas Aquinas, a thirteenth-century Dominican theologian, born just ten years after the Fourth Lateran Council, wrote extensively and incisively on the Eucharistic mystery. But the Eucharist was, for Aquinas, much more than merely a topic of academic interest; it was the center of

---

17. Innocent III, *Cum Marthae circa*, November 29, 1202, in Heinrich Denzinger et al., *Compendium of Creeds, Definitions, and Declarations on Matters of Faith and Morals*, 43rd ed. (San Francisco: Ignatius Press, 2012), no. 784, 259.

18. Denzinger et al., no. 802, 267.

his spiritual life. Thomas would typically celebrate Mass every day and would then assist at another Mass immediately afterward. Rarely, his contemporaries report, would he get through the liturgy without tears, so great was his identification with the unfolding of the Paschal Mystery. When he was wrestling with a particularly thorny intellectual question, he would pray before the Blessed Sacrament, frequently resting his head on the tabernacle itself, begging for inspiration. At the prompting of Pope Urban VIII, Thomas composed a magnificent series of poems and hymns for the newly instituted Feast of Corpus Christi, several of which are still in wide use today in the Catholic liturgy. Finally, one of the most mysterious events in Aquinas' life centered around the Eucharist. After he had completed his lengthy treatment of the Eucharist in the *Summa theologiae,* Thomas, still unsure whether he had spoken correctly or even adequately of the sacrament, placed the text at the foot of the crucifix and commenced to pray. According to the well-known legend, a voice came from the cross, "You have written well of me, Thomas. What would you have as a reward?" To which Aquinas responded, "Non nisi te, Domine" (Nothing but you, Lord).[19]

In this section, I would like to study in some detail that treatise which Aquinas placed before the Lord, for in many ways it sums up and gives pointed expression to the tradition that we have been surveying, and it became a permanent touchstone for much of the Catholic Eucharistic theology that followed it. It constitutes questions 73–83 of the third part of the *Summa theologiae,* Thomas' late-career masterpiece. But in order to understand his treatment of the key sacrament adequately, we have to glance, however briefly, at questions 60–63, which deal with the nature of a sacrament in general. Sacraments, Aquinas tells us, are types of signs, since they point to something that lies beyond them—namely, the sacred power that flows from the Passion of Christ. They

---

19. *Ystoria sancti Thome de Aquino de Guillaume de Tocco* (1323), ed. Claire le Brun-Gouanvic (Ontario: Pontifical Institute of Medieval Studies, 1996), 162.

are composed of a material element—oil, water, bread, wine, etc.—and a formal element, embodied in the words that accompany them. Thus, Baptism is a sacred sign involving the pouring of water and the uttering of the words, "I baptize you in the name of the Father, and of the Son, and of the Holy Spirit," the words specifying the sacred power of Christ operative in and through the water. We can see, therefore, that sacraments are not only signs of grace, but actually the instrumental causes of grace. In Thomas' curt language: "They cause what they signify."[20] The salvific energy of Christ's cross flows, as it were, through these sacred signs, much in the way that the power of the builder flows through the saw that he employs or the authority of the general is made manifest in the soldiers whom he commands.

With that general background in mind, we can turn now to the questions dealing specifically with the Eucharist. In the first article of question 73, Thomas poses the straightforward query whether the Eucharist should be called a sacrament. His answer situates the Eucharist very much in the context of the sacred banquet. All sacraments, he says, are designed to place the spiritual life within human beings, and the spiritual life is symbolically conformed to bodily life. Thus, just as food and drink are required for the sustenance of biological life, so the Eucharist is necessary for the sustenance of the life of grace. Precisely as *spirituale alimentum* (spiritual food), the Eucharist is thus placed in the genus of sacrament.[21] By it, the power of Christ's death and Resurrection flows into us like food into the digestive system. Commenting on the use of the term *communio* (communion) in regard to the Eucharist, Thomas says that through the sacrament we commune with Christ, participating in his flesh and divinity, and inasmuch as we share in Christ, we commune with one another through him.[22] I can't imagine a more succinct summary of the theme of the sacred meal.

---

20. Thomas Aquinas, *Summa theologiae* 3.62.1.
21. Thomas Aquinas, 3.73.1 (Leon. 12:138).
22. Thomas Aquinas, 3.73.4 (Leon. 12:142).

In question 75, Aquinas broaches the issue of the manner of Christ's Real Presence in the Eucharist. The complexity and thoroughness of his treatment shows that this subject, above all, preoccupied the greatest of the medieval theologians. Article 1 of question 75 poses the central issue bluntly enough: "Whether the body of Christ be in this sacrament in very truth, or merely in a figure or sign?" Let us attend to Thomas' response with some care. He first observes that the true Body and Blood (*verum corpus Christi et sanguinem*) are in the Eucharistic sacrament but not in such a way as to be apprehended by the senses; they are "visible" only through faith, which rests upon the divine authority.[23] We recall that many of the Church Fathers emphasized the importance of Christ's *words* in the determination of the Real Presence. By stressing our faith in the authority of Jesus, Thomas Aquinas is making much the same point. In his lovely hymn "Adoro Te Devote," Aquinas expressed this idea in a more poetic vein: "Seeing, touching, tasting are in thee deceived; / How says trusty hearing? That shall be believed."[24] Next, he tries to show how *conveniens* (fitting) it is that Christ is present in this sacrament in a qualitatively different way than in the others. The sacrifices of the old Law were, he says, prefigurations of the final sacrifice offered on Christ's cross; therefore, it follows that there should be *aliquid plus* (something more) in the sacrifice instituted by Jesus. And this something more is that the Eucharist contains *ipsum passum* (the one himself who suffered) and not simply a sign or indication of him.[25] In other words, if we were to say that Jesus is merely signified in the Eucharist, that sacrament would not be, in a qualitative sense, greater than any of the signs of God's presence described in the Old Testament or acted out in the rituals of the temple. Secondly, the dense reality of Christ's Eucharistic presence is fitting due to the intensity of Jesus' love. Aristotle said that the supreme sign of friendship is to want

---

23. Thomas Aquinas, 3.75.1 (Leon. 12:156).
24. "Adoro Te Devote," trans. Gerard Manley Hopkins, in *Ignatian Collection* (Park Ridge, IL: Word on Fire Classics, 2020), 285.
25. Thomas Aquinas, *Summa theologiae* 3.75.1 (Leon. 12:156).

to live together with one's friends, and this is just what Jesus makes possible by giving us his very self in the Eucharist. The night before he died, Jesus told his disciples, "I do not call you servants any longer. . . . I have called you friends" (John 15:15). Thomas implies that the Real Presence in the Eucharist is the seal and guarantee of that friendship with all the Lord's disciples across the ages.[26]

The third objection to this question is worth examining. The objector states that nobody can be simultaneously in many places. But the Body of Christ is present at the same time on many altars and in heaven. Therefore, the presence spoken of in the sacramental context must be merely a sign or a figure of the "real" one in heaven. In responding to this dilemma—which goes right back to Berengarius—Thomas makes a decisive distinction between Christ's bodily presence according to his "proper species" and that same bodily presence according to a species appropriate to the sacrament: a "sacramental species." "Proper species" is technical jargon for the ordinary appearance of something.[27] Thus, in his proper species, Christ is an embodied person of a particular height, weight, and color, existing "in" heaven, though we're not quite sure what this existence is like in a transcendent dimensional system. But this same embodied Christ can also become present according to a species, or appearance, that is alien to him—that is to say, according to a sacramental mode. In light of this distinction, Aquinas clarifies that the body of Christ is not in the sacrament of the Eucharist the way a body is ordinarily in a place, measured by its own dimensions and circumscribed by the contours of the space that it occupies. And thus, though we can say that Christ's body is on various altars at the same time, we shouldn't say that he is in various *places* at the same time, for this would be to confuse proper and sacramental modes of appearance. In a similar vein, Aquinas specifies that we shouldn't speak of carrying around the body of Christ when we process with the Eucharist or of

---

26. Thomas Aquinas, 3.75.1.
27. Thomas Aquinas, 3.75.1 ad 3.

imprisoning Jesus when we put the sacramental elements in the tabernacle. To do so would be to conflate these two basic modes of presence.
And this is why Thomas Aquinas and the mainstream of the Catholic
tradition remain uneasy with that section of the anti-Berengarian oath
that speaks of crunching Christ's body with one's teeth. In Aquinas'
more precise language, when one consumes the Eucharist, one crunches
the accidents of the bread with the teeth, not the body of Christ, since
Christ is being received substantially but according to his sacramental
species, not his proper species.[28]

This distinction helps to clear up a perhaps lingering doubt. At the
outset of his analysis, Thomas said that sacraments are found in the
genus of sign. So then, if the Eucharist is a sacrament, why should he
balk at characterizing it as a sign or figure of the body of Christ? As we
saw, a sign is that which points beyond itself to something else. This
is true of the Eucharist inasmuch as the sacramental species of Christ
indicates Christ in his proper species; there is still therefore a play of
presence and absence in the Eucharist. Nevertheless, this particular
sign has the unique capacity to contain perfectly (though hiddenly)
that toward which it points. Whereas the other sacraments contain
only the power of Christ (as we saw), the Eucharist uniquely contains
Christ himself, in the full reality of his presence. And thus it is the
chief of the sacramental signs.

Now, I realize that my reader might still be wondering how these
distinctions really *explain* anything. Do they tell us *how* Christ is
really present, when all the sensible evidence is that bread and wine
are still rather massively there. Aquinas realized the pertinence of such
questions, and this is why, in article 4 of question 75, he took up the
language of the Fourth Lateran Council and attempted to articulate
the Eucharistic change in terms of substance and accident. The specific
question that he posed was the following: whether bread can be
changed into the body of Christ. Having denied, for obvious reasons,

---

28. See Thomas Aquinas, 3.76.1.

that the change could be through some sort of ordinary local motion (the bread leaving and the body of Christ arriving), Thomas claims that the change takes place at the level of substance, that underlying and essentially invisible substrate that constitutes the deepest identity of a given thing. The substances of the bread and wine change into the substances of the Body and Blood of Jesus, even while the accidents (appearances) of bread and wine remain. This change, unlike anything that occurs in nature, is due to the extraordinary intensity of the divine power, which can reach, as it does in the act of creation, to the very roots of reality. The same God who made bread and wine from nothing and sustains them in existence from moment to moment, can transform the deepest ontological centers of those things into something else. Then how do we explain the perdurance of the accidents, once their proper substances have been changed? Once again, Thomas invokes the divine power.[29] Though God customarily sustains accidents through their proper substances, he can, for his own purposes, suspend the secondary causality and sustain them directly himself. Joseph Ratzinger (Pope Benedict XVI) said that, at the Eucharistic change, the bread and wine lose their independence as creatures and become, through God's power, pure signs of Christ's presence. They no longer point to themselves in any relevant sense, for they have become utterly transparent to the Christ who makes himself manifest through them.[30]

If this talk of substance and accident still seems puzzling, I would suggest that we translate the terms into the more straightforward "reality" and "appearance." Practically every major philosopher of both the classical and modern periods makes some sort of distinction between what appears and what is. And we are familiar with this demarcation in our ordinary experience. For the most part, appearance and reality coincide ("If it looks like a duck, walks like a duck, and quacks like a duck . . ."); but there are many exceptions to that rule, times when we

---

29. Thomas Aquinas, 3.75.5.

30. *Joseph Ratzinger Collected Works*, vol. 2, *Theology of the Liturgy*, ed. Michael J. Miller, trans. John Saward et al. (San Francisco: Ignatius Press, 2014), 233.

feel compelled to say, "I know it looks that way, but appearances are deceptive." When one gazes at the moon from the vantage point of a speeding car, it can certainly appear as though the moon is moving rapidly across the sky, though we know that this is not in fact the case. Although it certainly looks as though the sun traverses the sky in the course of the day, we know that this is not true, in substance. Or when we look into the distant heavens on a clear night, and we see the tiny lights of the stars, it certainly seems that we are seeing something that is substantially there, but we know that this is false. In point of fact, we are looking into the distant past, for the light from those stars has reached our eyes only after traveling across many years. Or sometimes we make a judgment about someone's character based upon one encounter with him, only to discover, after coming to know him much better, that our original impression was quite false. We might subsequently tell a friend, "I know he can *seem* that way, but he's really not." What these ordinary examples demonstrate is that reality is never simply reducible to appearance and that, at times, the deepest truth of things is revealed, not through what we see, but by what we hear from authoritative voices: a scientist, an astronomer, an experienced friend. Thomas Aquinas is arguing that, at the Eucharist, the appearances of bread and wine do not tell the deepest truth about what is really present and that, in point of fact, the authoritative word of Christ does.

Let us return to Ratzinger's point. In light of his clarification, we can appreciate the eschatological significance of the doctrine of transubstantiation. The Eucharistic elements, fruit of the earth and the work of human hands, are not destroyed or annihilated through the power of Christ; rather, they are transfigured, elevated into vehicles for Christ's self-communication. In the letters of Paul, we find the mysterious observations that, at the culmination of the present age, God will be "all in all" (1 Cor. 15:28) and that all people will come together in forming "the measure of the full stature of Christ" (Eph. 4:13). Could it be that the Eucharistic elements, transubstantiated into the Body and Blood of Jesus, are proleptic signs even now of what Christ intends for the whole of the universe? Could it be that, in them, we can see, however indistinctly, God's purpose in regard to even the humblest features of his creation? Perhaps, in light of this doctrine, we can begin to understand the mysterious words of Pierre Teilhard de Chardin that the Real Presence of Christ in the Eucharist signals the eschatological *transsubstantiation du monde* (the transubstantiation of the world).[31]

Having explored the nature of the Eucharist, Thomas finally endeavors to explain its effects. The principal consequence of the Eucharist is grace, or a share in the divine life. Since it contains *ipse Christus* (Christ himself) and since Christ came into the world as the bearer of God's life, the Eucharist, above any other sacrament or sign, contains and causes grace.[32] This is powerfully symbolized, Thomas suggests, in the appearances of bread and wine that remain after the transubstantiation. Just as food sustains, repairs, and delights the body, so the Eucharist sustains, repairs, and delights the soul.[33] Without the Body and Blood of Christ, in other words, the spiritual life in us would be compromised by sin, become atrophied and flattened out, and finally would fade away altogether. In article 4 of question 79, Thomas asks whether the Eucharist remits venial sin, and he answers in terms of this master metaphor of food and drink. Just as food restores to the body that which is lost through everyday effort, so the Eucharist restores that which is drained away from us spiritually through ordinary, day-to-day sins. "Something is also lost daily of our spirituality from the heat of concupiscence through venial sins, which lessen the fervor of charity."[34] Since it is Christ himself, who is nothing but the divine love, the Eucharist reignites in us that lost fervor; in short, it remits venial sin. We recall here the story of the conversion of Matthew. To the sacred

---

31. See Pierre Teilhard de Chardin, *The Divine Milieu*, ed. and trans. Bernard Wall et al. (New York: Harper & Row, 1965), 125.

32. Thomas Aquinas, *Summa theologiae* 3.79.1–2 (Leon. 12:221).

33. Thomas Aquinas, 3.79.1.

34. Thomas Aquinas, 3.79.4.

banquet Jesus invited the sinful Matthew, and then in his wake there arrived a whole crowd of Matthew's partners in crime. The Eucharistic meal is the place where sinners are especially welcome, for it is the place where they will find precisely what they need. Why then, we might wonder, does Thomas contend that the Eucharist ought not to be received by someone in the state of mortal sin? By definition, mortal sin is a wrong that has so radically compromised one's relation to God that it has effectively killed the divine life in the one who commits it. Therefore, just as it would be foolish to give medicine to a dead person, it would be counterindicated, Thomas concludes, to offer the healing power of the Eucharist to one who is spiritually dead. In saying this, of course, he is only reiterating what St. Paul said to the Christians at Corinth. Commenting on those who receive the Eucharist unworthily, Paul said that they "eat and drink judgment against themselves" (1 Cor. 11:29).

I would like to say a word about the properly delightful quality of the Eucharist of which Thomas speaks. Even the dullest and least appetizing fare would suffice for the maintenance of life; but who among us doesn't enjoy a tasty and sensually appealing meal? So the Eucharist—in its sumptuous liturgical setting, surrounded by music, art, the Word of God, and the prayer of the community—does more than sustain the divine life in us. It delights us, as a foretaste of the heavenly banquet. And doesn't Babette's feast come to mind in this context?

Some Contemporary Approaches to the Real Presence

Thomas Aquinas' synthetic approach to the Eucharist, which drew together the scriptural and patristic witness along with the finest philosophical insight of the time, proved a formidable intellectual edifice. Though it was challenged by the Protestant Reformers in the sixteenth century, it was, in its essential structure, reaffirmed by the Council of Trent and successfully propagated through Catholic universities, seminaries, and pulpits well into modern times. It was only around the middle of the twentieth century that it was seriously challenged by Catholic theologians. Some complained that the focus on the category of substance led to an overly "thingified" understanding of the Eucharist, one that underplayed the dynamic and participative dimension of the sacrament. Others felt that the hyperstress on "real" presence led to an undervaluing of Christ's presence in other aspects of the liturgy and the life of the Church. Still others worried that the constant reiteration of Thomas' doctrine led to a furthering of the rupture between Catholics and Protestants. Finally, and most importantly, some scholars disputed whether the idea of substance itself was philosophically coherent. In light of the discoveries of contemporary chemistry and physics, did it still make sense, they wondered, to speak about the Eucharist in terms of Aristotelian philosophy?

All of these concerns conduced toward a radical re-thinking and re-presentation of the Church's Eucharistic faith. Certain theologians began to use the terms "transignification" and "transfinalization" in place of the traditional "transubstantiation." By the first they meant the fundamental shift in meaning that occurs in the Eucharistic context, whereby the bread and wine come to signify, in the midst of the community's ritual prayer, the body and blood of Jesus. By the second, they meant the change in the end or finality of the Eucharistic elements when they are prayed over at Mass: now they are no longer merely for the purpose of nourishing the body or expressing the oneness of the community; rather, their deepest purpose is to point to Christ and the eschatological fulfillment of the Church. These approaches—relatively psychological, symbolic, subjectivistic—avoided the physicalism of which we just spoke and seemed to make the Eucharistic mystery more accessible to a modern audience. However, almost immediately, strong objections were raised. Many of the critics of transignification and transfinalization saw the new theories as simply slightly revised versions of the discredited Berengarian explanation. If the Eucharistic change involves only a shift in the meaning that the worshiping community assigns to the bread and wine, then the dense objectivity of Christ's presence seemed fatally compromised. If it were only a matter of a given community "deeming" the bread and wine to be something else (much as Americans deem a tri-colored cloth to be representative of the nation), then the community would come to control the Eucharist rather than vice versa. In his encyclical letter *Mysterium Fidei,* Pope Paul VI acknowledged a limited legitimacy to the new language, but insisted that any change in meaning and finality had to be rooted in a more elemental change in being, hence in a transubstantiation.[35]

In the wake of this debate, a number of theologians put forward, with the help of both biblical scholarship and contemporary philosophical research, a theory that reconciled the classical teaching with the best elements of the new approach. Much of this centered around a consideration of the power of the divine word. The philosophers J.L. Austin and Ludwig Wittgenstein reminded us that our words can function, not only descriptively, but performatively as well. On the one hand, the words "that house is blue" indicate a state of affairs, but the words "You're fired," when uttered by one's superior, do not simply point out what is the case; they change what is the case. Similarly, if a properly uniformed and deputed officer of the law were to say to you, "You're under arrest," you would, in fact, be under arrest, precisely through the power of his pronouncement. Or if a properly designated umpire were to shout, "You're out!" as a Major League Baseball player slid into third base, the unfortunate player would, whether he liked it or not, be out, the umpire's verbal expression having objectively changed the flow of the game. We can, in Austin's famous phrase, "do things with words."[36]

---

35. Paul VI, *Mysterium Fidei* (1965).

36. J.L. Austin, *How to Do Things with Words*, 2nd. ed. (Cambridge, MA: Harvard University Press, 1975).

In light of this clarification about the performative quality of human words, theologians began to consider anew the power of the divine word. In the book of Genesis, we hear that creation occurred through a series of divine speech-acts: "God said, 'Let there be light,' and there was light. . . . God said, 'Let the waters under the sky be gathered together into one place, and let the dry land appear.' And it was so. . . . And God said, 'Let the earth bring forth living creatures of every kind: cattle and creeping things and wild animals of the earth of every kind.' And it was so" (Gen. 1:3, 9, 24). God is not describing a preexisting state of affairs; he is, through his speech, bringing things into being. St. John, of course, reiterates this idea when in the prologue to his Gospel he says, "In the beginning was the Word. . . . He was in the beginning with God. All things came into being through him, and without him not one thing came to be" (John 1:1–3). In the book of the prophet Isaiah, we find the same idea expressed in beautifully poetic form. Speaking the words of Yahweh, Isaiah says, "For as the rain and the snow come down from heaven, and do not return there until they have watered the earth . . . so shall my word be that goes out from my mouth; it shall not return to me empty, but it shall accomplish that which I purpose, and succeed in the thing for which I sent it" (Isa. 55:10–11). Again, in the biblical reading, God's word does not so much describe as *achieve.* Thomas Aquinas gave more philosophical expression to this notion when he said that God does not know things because they exist (as we do) but rather that things exist because God knows them. Contemporary Jesuit theologian Karl Rahner summed up this line of thought, commenting, "The word of God is the salutary word which brings with it what it affirms."[37]

Now, that very word by which God creates the cosmos became incarnate in Jesus of Nazareth: "And the Word became flesh and lived among us" (John 1:14). This means that Jesus is (as we have already

---

37. Karl Rahner, *More Recent Writings*, trans. Kevin Smyth, Theological Investigations, vol. 4 (Baltimore: Helicon, 1966), 259–260.

indicated) not simply a holy man whose words describe God; he is himself the divine word which affects what it says. And so at the height of a terrible storm on the Sea of Galilee, Jesus stood up in the boat, "rebuked the wind, and said to the sea, 'Peace! Be still!'" and "the wind ceased, and there was a dead calm" (Mark 4:39). And standing before the tomb of his friend who had been interred for four days, Jesus said in a loud voice, "Lazarus, come out," and "the dead man came out, his hands and feet bound with strips of cloth, and his face wrapped in a cloth" (John 11:43–44). And kneeling in front of a small girl lying dead in her room, Jesus said, "'Talitha cum,' which means, 'Little girl, get up!' And immediately the girl got up and began to walk about" (Mark 5:41–42). Again and again, the Gospel writers show us how Jesus' words are efficacious and transformative, producing what they pronounce. Again and again, they present Jesus himself as the incarnation of the creative word of Genesis and of that Isaian word which does not return without accomplishing its purpose. The night before he died, Jesus performed his most extraordinary word-act. Gathered with the Twelve for a Passover supper, he "took bread, said the blessing, broke it, and giving it to his disciples, he said, 'Take and eat; this is my body.' Then he took a cup, gave thanks, and gave it to them, saying, 'Drink from it, all of you, for this is my blood of the covenant, which will be shed on behalf of many for the forgiveness of sins'" (Matt. 26:26–28). If he were an ordinary prophet or teacher, these powerful words, spoken the night before his death, would have burned themselves into the consciousness of his followers and carried enormous symbolic resonance. They might even have changed his disciples profoundly at the spiritual and psychological level. But Jesus was not one prophet among many; he was the incarnate Word of God. Therefore, his words had the power to create, to affect reality at the deepest possible level. Since what he says *is,* the words "this is my body" and "this is my blood" effectively change the bread and wine into his Body and Blood. Like all divine utterances, they *produce* what they say. The same Word that spoke the elements of bread and wine into existence in the first place now speaks them into a new mode of being, changing them into the bearers of Christ's sacramental presence.

For Catholic theology, this efficacious word of Christ has not passed out of existence or evanesced into a vague historical memory. Rather, it endures in the Church: in its preaching, its teaching, its sacraments, and above all in the Eucharistic liturgy. When the priest at Mass greets the people, he does not do so in his own name, and when he preaches, he is not sharing his private opinions. In both cases, he is allowing the Word of Jesus to speak through his words. Nowhere is this transparency of the priest clearer than when he prays the so-called "institution narrative" at the heart of the Eucharistic Prayer. Addressing God the Father, he recalls what Jesus did the night before he died: Jesus "took bread and, giving thanks, broke it, and gave it to his disciples. . . . In a similar way, Jesus took the chalice and, once more giving thanks, he gave it to his disciples. . ." But then he slips into the very words of Jesus: "This is *my* Body, which will be given up for you. . . . This is the chalice of *my* Blood, the Blood of the new and eternal covenant."[38] At that moment, the consecrating priest is most fully acting *in persona Christi* (in the person of Christ), effacing himself utterly and permitting the same divine word that transformed bread and wine long ago to transform them now.

What happens, therefore (and here we see the value of the newer approaches), is that the bread and wine have indeed been transignified and transfinalized, but the shift in meaning has not happened through any puny human effort but through the divine word. And this entails, as we've been arguing, a change at the level of being. In this precise sense, then, transignification and transubstantiation do indeed coincide. Rahner points out that the traditional teaching of the Church confirms this coincidence when it reminds us that the Real Presence of Christ in the Eucharist is a consequence of the power of the word.

---

38. *Roman Missal* (ICEL, 2010) (emphasis added).

The Council of Florence says expressly that "the form of this sacrament [the Eucharist] is the words of the Savior with which he *effected* [*made*] this sacrament," and the Council of Trent says that Christ becomes present in the Eucharistic elements *ex vi verborum* (by the power of the words).[39] Rahner specifies that even the Eucharistic elements, preserved in the tabernacle for Adoration, would not really be the sacramental species if they were not being constantly determined by the words of consecration, the words of explanation, which were pronounced over them.[40] Even in the silence of the tabernacle, a divine word is being spoken.

One of the most insightful contemporary commentators on the Eucharist is the Catholic philosopher Robert Sokolowski, and I would like to conclude this section with a brief consideration of his subtle reflections on the Real Presence.[41] Sokolowski argues that there are three ways to think about the relationship between spirit and matter. According to the first, which he calls "Darwinian," matter is really all that there is, and what we call "spirit" is simply an epiphenomenon of matter. In this Darwinian reading, mind and will, for example, are only refined brain functions. A second way to understand the relationship between the two realities is what he characterizes as the "Aristotelian." In this view, spirit and matter exist more or less side by side and interact with one another in complex ways. Think, for instance, of the standard view of how body and soul relate to each other. But the third model, which Sokolowski calls "creationist" or "biblical," holds to the precedence of spirit over matter. According to this mode of interpretation, the properly spiritual—mind and will—preceded matter and can determine matter according to its

---

39. Denzinger et al., *Compendium of Creeds, Definitions, and Declarations*, no. 1321, 341; no. 1640, 394 (emphasis added).

40. Rahner, *More Recent Writings*, 284.

41. Robert Sokolowski, *Christian Faith and Human Understanding: Studies on the Eucharist, Trinity, and the Human Person* (Washington, DC: The Catholic University of America Press, 2006), 101–104.

purposes. Everything we said above about creation through the word is intelligible only in the context of this third framework. Problems occur in Eucharistic theology, Sokolowski maintains, when we try to think about the Eucharist in the context of either of the first two models. Within a Darwinian framework, the Real Presence is just so much nonsense, for matter is all that there is. Within an Aristotelian framework, the Real Presence comes to be thought of as a sort of inner-worldly change, some new and unprecedented way for finite natures—one spiritual and the other material—to relate to one another. But within the biblical context, things can make a bit more sense, for in this reading, God is not one nature among others, one being within the world, but rather the creator of the world, the ground of all finite things. And thus God can relate to matter in a noncompetitive way, becoming present through it, without undermining it. The supreme instance of this noncompetitive involvement of God within creation is, of course, the Incarnation, and the Eucharist is nothing but a sacramental prolongation of the Incarnation. Thus, God can use the material as a vehicle for his presence, without ceasing to be God and without overwhelming the matter that he uses. The Eucharist does not involve the supplanting of one finite nature by another—as though a tree becomes a leopard but continues to look and react like a tree—but the noncompetitive presence of God within an aspect of the nature that he has made. Thus, concludes Sokolowski, when the Church speaks of Christ being substantially present in the Eucharist even as the material appearances of bread and wine remain, it is assuming this uniquely biblical perspective on the relation of spirit and matter.

Both Rahner and Sokolowski maintain that the Real Presence in the Eucharist is dependent, finally, on the power of the Creator God. It is only through the word of this reality that lies outside of the limitations of the finite world that the Eucharistic change is possible. And it is precisely to this God, made manifest in the

Incarnation and the Eucharist, that St. John, St. Irenaeus, St. John Chrysostom, Origen, Lanfranc, and St. Thomas Aquinas bore such eloquent witness.

"Here We Have No Lasting City"

Earlier in this chapter, we saw that many of the Church Fathers characterized the Eucharist as food that effectively immortalizes those who consume it. They understood that if Christ is really present in the Eucharistic elements, the one who eats and drinks the Lord's Body and Blood becomes configured to Christ in a far more than metaphorical way. The Eucharist, they concluded, Christifies and hence eternalizes. Now, again, if the Eucharist were no more than a symbol, this kind of language would be so much nonsense. But if the doctrine of the Real Presence is true, then this literal eternalization of the recipient of communion must be maintained.

But what does this transformation practically entail? It implies that the whole of one's life—body, psyche, emotions, spirit—becomes ordered to the eternal dimension, to the realm of God. It means that one's energies and interests, one's purposes and plans, are lifted out of a purely temporal context and given an entirely new spiritual valence. The Christified person knows that his life is not finally about him but about God; the Eucharistized person understands that her treasure is to be found above and not below. Wealth, pleasure, power, honor, success, titles, degrees, even friendships and family connections are all relativized as the high adventure of life with God opens up. The eternalized person can say with Paul, "It is no longer I who live, but it is Christ who lives in me" (Gal. 2:20), and "Here we have no lasting city" (Heb. 13:14).

The paradox is this: such a reconfiguration actually makes such people more rather than less effective and happy in this world. G.K. Chesterton said that when he was an agnostic and was convinced that he could be happy only through the use of this world's goods, he was actually miserable. But when he realized that he was not meant to be finally satisfied here below—when he was eternalized through the Eucharist—he found, to his infinite surprise, that he became happy. Dorothy Day, the founder of the Catholic Worker movement, was one of the twentieth century's most radical advocates of social justice and peace—and this was *because* she was so passionately devoted to the Eucharist, *because* she had been, body and soul, immortalized through consuming the Real Presence of Jesus.

This is why I tell people to be very careful when they approach the Eucharist. Were the elements simply symbols—inventions of our own spiritual creativity and desire—they would pose no particular threat. But since they are the power and presence of God, they will change the one who consumes them. When the communicant says "Amen" and receives the proffered host and chalice, he'd better be prepared to live an eternal life.

Epilogue

THE EMMAUS SUPPER

.

W e began with a consideration of "Babette's Feast," a story in which the Eucharistic themes of meal, sacrifice, and Real Presence are beautifully evoked. I should like to close with a meditation on another story with powerful Eucharistic resonances, one that comes from the earliest stratum of the Christian tradition and that speaks compellingly of those same motifs. The twenty-fourth chapter of the Gospel of Luke is a literary masterpiece, but the narrative of the encounter on the road to Emmaus is, as N.T. Wright pointed out, a masterpiece within the masterpiece. It is, with the possible exception of the sixth chapter of John's Gospel, the most thorough and important New Testament meditation on the meaning of the Eucharist.

The story commences with two people walking the wrong way: "Now on that same day two of them were going to a village called Emmaus, about seven miles from Jerusalem" (Luke 24:13). The entire momentum of Luke's Gospel is in the direction of Jerusalem. It is to that city that Jesus sets his face; it is there that he cleanses the temple, celebrates his Last Supper, does battle with the enemies of Israel, rises from the dead; and it is there that he sends the Holy Spirit for the formation of the Church. Jerusalem is "Mt. Zion, true pole of the earth" (Ps. 48:2 Grail) to which all the tribes of the Lord are called. Therefore, these two erstwhile followers of Jesus, heading away from the holy city, are going decidedly in the wrong direction. As they walked, they were joined by Jesus himself, though they were prevented from recognizing him. This lack of recognition is a typical motif in the Resurrection stories. There seems to have been something odd, uncanny, unfamiliar about the risen Lord. In Matthew's account of the Great Commission, we hear that some of them fell down and worshiped the risen Christ, while some others doubted. And in John's story of the appearance by the seaside, we are told that "none of the disciples dared to ask him, 'Who are you?' because they knew it was the Lord" (John 21:12). And of course, Mary Magdalene, seeing Jesus on Easter morning, thought he was the gardener. Only when he spoke her name, "Mary," did she recognize him (John 20:16). Though the figure they saw was clearly the same Jesus whom they had known, there was some discontinuity between the pre-Resurrection and post-Resurrection Christ. It was Jesus, but he was somehow else; he was in this world but rather dramatically not of it. This hiddenness is on display in the Emmaus story. But there is another reason for their lack of recognition: they don't see because their lives are misdirected. Seeing correctly and living correctly are correlated; vision and discipleship are mutually implicative.

The precise nature of their confusion is revealed in their wonderfully ironic conversation with Christ. With delicious faux innocence, Jesus inquires, "What are you discussing with each other while you walk along?" (Luke 24:17). Looking downcast, one of the disciples, Cleopas by name, commences to recite all of the data concerning Jesus of Nazareth: he was a prophet mighty in word and deed before God and all the people; he was handed over by the chief priests and crucified; they had hoped he would be the redeemer of Israel; some women have even reported that he was risen from the dead. Everything he says is correct, but his deep unhappiness proves that he has grasped the meaning of none of it. He is like someone who has heard every word of a joke, but doesn't "get it" and hence can't laugh. Then the stranger speaks: "Oh, how foolish you are, and how slow of heart to believe all that the prophets have declared! Was it not necessary that the Messiah should suffer these things and then enter into his glory?" (Luke 24:25–26). Jesus then rehearsed for them the whole of the biblical story, showing how it culminated in the Messiah who offered a sacrifice for the salvation of the world. He demonstrated, we presume, that the narrative commencing with Adam and Eve, continuing through Abraham, Isaac, Jacob, Moses, David, Isaiah, and Jeremiah, centered around and pointed to a sacrificial love so complete that, by it, the effects of sin are undone.

When they came near the village to which they were heading, the stranger "gave the impression that he was going on farther" (Luke 24:28), but they pressed him to stay. Then, sitting down with them for table fellowship, Jesus "took bread, said the blessing, broke it, and gave it to them." Repeating the great gestures of the Last Supper, Jesus made present for them again the sacrifice of the cross, the act by which he offered his own body as reparation for the sins of the world. In short, he wove together the themes of the sacred banquet and the sacrifice that made the banquet possible, summing up thereby the story of Israel that he had narrated on the road. And at that moment, when the Scriptures and the meal and the sacrifice came together as a coherent whole, they recognized him; he became really present to them. At that moment, they "got" him; they understood how all of the aspects of his life fit together; they *saw* him. And in the next instant, he disappeared.

Once they saw, they moved, this time in the right direction. Despite the lateness of the hour, despite the dangers of the road, despite the persecution that awaited them in the holy city, they got up immediately and raced to Jerusalem. There they joined the eleven Apostles, the other witnesses of the Resurrection, the seed of the Church, gathered on the top of Mt. Zion. They heard the good news, "the Lord has risen indeed, and he has appeared to Simon!" (Luke 24:34). And then they shared their "god spell" that Jesus had made himself known to them "in the breaking of the bread," New Testament shorthand for the Eucharist (24:35).

As many commentators have pointed out over the centuries, this narrative is a symbolic presentation of the liturgy. We come to Mass, like these two disciples, often walking in the wrong direction. This is why we beg, in the Kyrie Eleison, for the forgiveness of our sins. But Jesus, with infinite patience, comes to join us, opening up for us the meaning of the Scriptures, showing us once again how the Old Testament story culminates in and centers around him. This is the Liturgy of the Word. Though this illumination is necessary, it is not sufficient. We don't fully understand who Jesus is until we sit down with him at the sacred, sacrificial banquet that makes present his saving cross. In the Liturgy of the Eucharist, in the breaking of the bread and the drinking of the cup, we see him in his Real Presence. Finally, having seen, we move, presumably in a more correct direction. At the close of the liturgy, we are sent: "Go forth, the Mass is ended." Hans Urs von Balthasar said that Jesus vanished immediately after being recognized by the two Emmaus disciples because he disappears into the mission of the Church. So the Eucharistic Christ becomes our mission, our work.

Throughout this book we have traced the Eucharistic themes of banquet, sacrifice, and Real Presence. The Emmaus story—which we relive at every Mass—demonstrates how tightly interwoven these motifs are. The sacrificed Christ makes the messianic banquet possible—and it is at that banquet that we feast on his Flesh, which is real food, and on his Blood, which is real drink.

Bibliography

Ambrose of Milan. *On the Mysteries*. Translated by H. De Romestin. In *Nicene and Post-Nicene Fathers of the Christian Church,* Second Series, edited by Philip Schaff and Henry Wace, vol. 10, *Ambrose: Select Works and Letters*, 315–325. Buffalo, NY: Christian Literature Publishing Co., 1896. NewAdvent.org.

Anselm. *Cur Deus Homo*. In *Anselm: Basic Writings*, edited and translated by Thomas Williams, 237–326. Indianapolis, IN: Hackett, 2007.

Aristotle. *The Nicomachean Ethics*. Translated by Robert C. Bartlett and Susan D. Collins. Chicago: University of Chicago Press, 2011.

Augustine. *Commentary on the Lord's Sermon on the Mount with Seventeen Related Sermons*. Edited by Hermigild Dressler. Translated by Denis J. Kavanagh. Washington, DC: The Catholic University of America Press, 2010.

Austin, J.L. *How to Do Things with Words*. 2nd ed. Cambridge, MA: Harvard University Press, 1975.

Balthasar, Hans Urs von. *The Scandal of the Incarnation: Irenaeus Against the Heresies*. Translated by John Saward. San Francisco: Ignatius Press, 1990.

Berengarius of Tours. *Apologia*. In *Un testo inedito di Berengario di Tours e il Concilio Romano del 1079*. Edited by Martinio Matronola. Milan: Vita e Pensiero, 1936.

———. *De sacra coena adversus Lanfrancum*. Edited by Willem Hermanus Beekenkamp. The Hague: Martinus Nijhoff, 1941.

Bradshaw, Paul and Maxwell Johnson. *The Eucharistic Liturgies: Their Evolution and Interpretation*. Collegeville, MN: Liturgical Press, 2012.

Brown, Raymond E. *The Birth of the Messiah*. Garden City, NY: Image Books, 1977.

———. *The Gospel According to John I–XII*. New York: Doubleday, 1966.

Catechism of the Catholic Church. New York: Image Books, 1995.

Chesterton, G.K. *What's Wrong with the World*. New York: Dodd & Mead, 1910.

Cyril of Jerusalem. *Catechetical Lectures.* Translated by Edwin Hamilton Gifford. In *Nicene and Post-Nicene Fathers,* Second Series, edited by Philip Schaff and Henry Wace, 1–401. Buffalo, NY: Christian Literature Publishing Co., 1894. NewAdvent.org.

Day, Dorothy. *From Union Square to Rome.* Silver Spring, MD: Preservation of the Faith, 1938.

Denzinger, Heinrich and Peter Hünermann et al. eds. *Compendium of Creeds, Definitions, and Declarations on Matters of Faith and Morals.* 43rd ed. San Francisco: Ignatius Press, 2012.

Dinesen, Isak. "Babette's Feast." In *Anecdotes of Destiny and Ehrengard*, 19–59. New York: Vintage International, 1993.

Francis of Assisi. "Canticle of Brother Sun." In *Francis and Clare: The Complete Works*, translated by Regis J. Armstrong and Ignatius C. Brady, 37–39. Mahwah, NJ: Paulist Press, 1982.

Guillaume de Tocco. *Ystoria sancti Thome de Aquino.* Edited by Claire le Brun-Gouanvic. Ontario: Pontifical Institute of Medieval Studies, 1996.

Hahn, Scott and John Bergsma. "Covenant." In *The Oxford Encyclopedia of the Bible and Theology*, vol. 1, edited by Samuel E. Balentine, 155–166. Oxford: Oxford University Press, 2015.

Ignatius of Antioch. *Epistle to the Ephesians: Shorter and Longer Versions.* In *The Ante-Nicene Fathers: The Writings of the Fathers down to A.D. 325*, edited and translated by Alexander Roberts and James Donaldson, vol. 1, *The Apostolic Fathers—Justin Martyr—Irenaeus*, 49–58. Buffalo, NY: Christian Literature Publishing Co., 1885. NewAdvent.org.

———. *Epistle to the Romans: Shorter and Longer Versions.* In *The Ante-Nicene Fathers: The Writings of the Fathers down to A.D. 325*, edited and translated by Alexander Roberts and James Donaldson, vol. 1, *The Apostolic Fathers—Justin Martyr—Irenaeus*, 73–78. Buffalo, NY: Christian Literature Publishing Co., 1885. NewAdvent.org.

Innocent III, Pope. *Letter* Cum Marthae circa *to Archbishop John of John of Lyon.* November 29, 1202. In *Compendium of Creeds, Definitions, and Declarations on Matters of Faith and Morals*, 43rd ed., edited by Heinrich Denzinger et al., nos. 782–784. San Francisco, Ignatius Press, 2012.

Irenaeus. *Against Heresies.* In *The Ante-Nicene Fathers: The Writings of the Fathers down to A.D. 325*, edited and translated by Alexander Roberts and James Donaldson, vol. 1, *The Apostolic Fathers—Justin Martyr—Irenaeus*, 309–567. Buffalo, NY: Christian Literature Publishing Co., 1885. NewAdvent.org.

————. *Irenaeus on the Christian Faith: A Condensation of* Against Heresies. Translated and edited by James R. Payton Jr. Eugene, OR: Pickwick, 2011.

John Chrysostom. *In proditionem Judae*. In *Patrologiae cursus completus*, series Graeca prior, 49:373–392. Paris: J.-P. Migne, 1862.

John Paul II, Pope. *Ecclesia de Eucharistia*. April 17, 2003. Vatican.va.

Joseph Ratzinger. *Joseph Ratzinger: Collected Works*, vol. 2, *Theology of the Liturgy: The Sacramental Foundation of Christian Existence*. Edited by Michael J. Miller. Translated by John Saward, Kenneth Baker, Henry Taylor, et al. San Francisco, Ignatius Press, 2014.

Justin Martyr. *The First Apology*. In *The Ante-Nicene Fathers: The Writings of the Fathers down to A.D. 325*, edited and translated by Alexander Roberts and James Donaldson, vol. 1, *The Apostolic Fathers—Justin Martyr—Irenaeus*, 163–187. Buffalo, NY: Christian Literature Publishing Co., 1885. NewAdvent.org.

Leiva-Merikakis, Erasmo. *Fire of Mercy, Heart of the Word: Meditations on the Gospel According to St. Matthew*. 4 vols. San Francisco: Ignatius Press, 1996–2021.

Leo the Great, Pope. "Sermon 48." In *St. Leo the Great: Sermons*, translated by Jane Patricia Freeland and Agnes Josephine Conway, 205–209. *The Fathers of the Church: A New Translation*, vol. 93. Washington, DC: The Catholic University of America Press, 1996.

Levering, Matthew. *Sacrifice and Community: Jewish Offering and Christian Eucharist*. Malden, MA: Blackwell, 2005.

Lewis, C.S. *Mere Christianity*. New York: HarperCollins, 2001.

Newman, John Henry. *An Essay in Aid of a Grammar of Assent*. Notre Dame, IN: University of Notre Dame Press, 1979.

O'Connor, Flannery. *Flannery O'Connor Collection*. Park Ridge, IL: Word on Fire Classics, 2019.

————. *The Habit of Being: Letters of Flannery O'Connor*. Edited by Sally Fitzgerald. New York: Farrar, Straus, & Giroux, 1979.

Origen of Alexandria. "The Homilies on Exodus." In *Homilies on Genesis and Exodus*, translated by Ronald E. Heine, 227–387. Washington, DC: The Catholic University of America Press, 1982.

Paul VI, Pope. *Mysterium Fidei: Encyclical of Pope Paul VI on the Holy Eucharist*. September 3, 1965. Vatican.va.

Pelikan, Jaroslav. *The Christian Tradition: A History of the Development of Doctrine*, vol. 3, *The Growth of Medieval Theology (600–1300)*. Chicago: University of Chicago Press, 1978.

Plato. *The Symposium*. Translated by Alexander Nehama and Paul Woodruff. Indianapolis, IN: Hackett, 1989.

Pseudo-Dionysius. *The Divine Names*. In *Pseudo-Dionysius: The Complete Works*, translated by Colm Luibheid, 47–131. New York: Paulist Press, 1987.

Rahner, Karl. *More Recent Writings*. Translated by Kevin Smyth. Vol. 4 of Theological Investigations. Baltimore: Helicon, 1966.

Roman Missal. International Commission on English in the Liturgy, 2010.

Second Vatican Council. *Lumen Gentium: Dogmatic Constitution on the Church*. In *The Word on Fire Vatican II Collection*, 45–149. Park Ridge, IL: Word on Fire Institute, 2021.

Sokolowski, Robert. *Christian Faith and Human Understanding: Studies on the Eucharist, Trinity, and the Human Person*. Washington, DC: The Catholic University of America Press, 2006.

Teilhard de Chardin, Pierre. *The Divine Milieu*. Edited by Bernard Wall. Translated by Bernard Wall et al. New York: Harper & Row, 1965.

Thomas Aquinas. "Adoro Te Devote." Translated by Gerard Manley Hopkins. In *Ignatian Collection*, 285. Park Ridge, IL: Word on Fire Classics, 2020.

———. *Summa contra Gentiles*. Translated by Anton C. Pegis. New York: Hanover House, 1955.

———. *Summa theologiae*. In *Sancti Thomae de Aquino Opera omnia*. Leonine ed. Vols. 4–12. Rome, 1888–1906.

———. *Summa theologiae*. 2nd rev. ed. Translated by the Fathers of the English Dominican Province. New York: Benzinger, 1947. NewAdvent.org.

Wright, N.T. "Jesus and the Identity of God." *Ex Auditu* 14 (January 1998): 42–56.

———. *Simply Christian: Why Christianity Makes Sense*. New York: HarperOne, 2006.

Yeats, W.B. "The Second Coming." In *The Major Works: Including Poems, Plays, and Critical Prose*, edited by Edward Larrissy, 91. Oxford: Oxford University Press, 1997.

Index

Abraham
    and binding of Isaac, 51–52, 71
    covenant of, 49–52, 54, 57–59, 66,
        70
    Jesus as offspring of, 80
    in salvation history, 22, 48–49, 68,
        110
Adam
    and Jesus, 27–28, 30, 37
    as priest, 20
    in salvation history, 21–22, 24,
        47–48, 110
    as steward of creation, 20
Ambrose of Milan, 83–84
anamnesis, 67
Anselm, 64–65
anti-Berengarian oath, 87–88, 94
Aristotle, 40, 88, 92
ark of the covenant, 54
asceticism (extreme), 12
Atonement theology, 64
Augustine, 62, 83–84
Austin, J.L., 100

Babette's Feast
    and delightfulness of the Mass, 98
    and forgiveness, 70
    and Isaiah's feast, 25
    narrative (summary), 4–16
    and sacrifice, 46, 74
Babylonian exile, 55
barque of Peter, 36–37

Benedict XVI, Pope. *See* Ratzinger,
    Joseph
Berengarius of Tours, 80, 85–88, 93
Bible
    and anger of God, 46
    as Christ's speech, 40
    covenant theme of, 50
    faith in, 52
    and Gnosticism, 19
    and loop of grace, 30
    and Marcionism, 58
    and non-competitive God, 68
    and Real Presence, 74, 82, 84, 86
    and salvation history, 22, 47,
        110–111
    See also individual books of by
        name
Blixen, Karen. *See* Dinesen, Isak
blood, use in Hebrew sacrificial cult,
    53–56, 66, 69–70
blood consumption, Old Testament
    prohibitions of, 76–77
blood of the covenant, 16, 32, 65–66,
    82
Body and Blood of Christ
    as lifeblood of the Church, 2–3
    and Real Presence, 74, 77–89, 92,
        95, 97, 99, 102–103, 106, 111
    as sacred meal, 32–34, 41–43
    and sacrifice of Jesus, 14–16, 69–70,
        72
Brown, Raymond E., 27, 77n3

116

.